DO-IT-YOURSELF
FAMILY MONEY KIT

DO-IT-YOURSELF
FAMILY MONEY KIT
A Four-Step Method
To Building
Financial Security

Philip Rahney

Kimberly, Jones Publishing Company

Author's Note: Grateful acknowledgment Marty for your
in-depth manuscript review. Some of the names in this book
have been changed.

Library of Congress Cataloging in Publication Data

Rahney, Philip, 1943-
  Do-it-yourself family money kit.

  (A Family education book)
  Includes index.
  1. Finance, Personal. I. Title. II. Series.

HG179.R28   332.024   81-48000
ISBN 0-941412-00-8   AACR2
ISBN 0-941412-01-6 (pbk.)

Text copy set in 11 point Century Expanded typeface on
13 point leading for readability by Priesman Graphics, Omaha;
mechanicals by KJPC; cover design by Richard Whalen,
Priesman Graphics; book production by Inter-Collegiate Press,
Shawnee Mission, KS.

A Family Education Book

Manufactured in the United States of America

10 9 8 7 6 5 4 3 2 1

For Pat and Matthew

The beginning is the most important part of the work.
— Plato, *The Republic*

TABLE OF CONTENTS

INTRODUCTION

Few of us escaped childhood (adulthood?) without at least some experience with kit-building. Model cars, boats, planes, every imaginable replica of *the real thing* helped while away our summers and provided a sense of unsurpassed accomplishment for the hours of intricacy and dedication involved. But how many of us in our haste for posterity have tried disappointingly to replicate the finished product (remember the full-color picture on the kit container?) by foregoing the step-by-step instructions or omitting some of the parts altogether?

Financial security is like the full-color picture on the kit container: *it's what we envision our financial destiny to be.* It's the full-color picture of the good life, success, money in the bank, happiness, even (deja vu) posterity. For most of us, that picture has to be put together piece-by-piece, step-by-step. Assembled chaotically with no plan of action, that destiny will hold little resemblance to the true picture you envision and certainly deserve for yourself and your family.

This book contains all of the parts and instructions necessary to build a financially secure tomorrow — a tomorrow without money problems, without money worries. It's going to require time, dedication, and effort on your part to put it all together correctly, but the result — the full-color picture of your financial destiny — will provide that sense of accomplishment that only comes from a job done to the best of one's ability.

Unlike with model kit-building, don't wait for summertime or spare time to begin putting your "family money kit" together. Every day wasted is a day lost forever. You can — in reality, *you must* — do it yourself because no one is going to do it for you.

Pledge of Commitment

I, to the best of my ability, do hereby pledge to apply the principles of financial planning and money management methods described in this book toward building a better, more financially secure future for myself and my family.

CHAPTER ONE

THE FOUR BASIC STEPS TO BUILDING FINANCIAL SECURITY

OVERVIEW AND CHALLENGE

It would be difficult indeed to name anything more precious and desirable to the family than financial security. And yet, based on income estimates alone, many families who *should* be well-off are flirting on the brink of bankruptcy, while those who *should* be barely making ends meet are enjoying relative financial growth. Inconsistent and dilemmatic as this may seem, it is relatively easy to explain and the explanation dispels a common myth with respect to the concept of financial security.

Possessing a large income does not, in itself, assure security from money problems. Most would agree that it should, but a quick review of daily bankruptcy notices in local newspapers reveals a seemingly disproportionate number of such filings by "well-off" individuals. One possible reason for this is the commonly held but fallacious belief that a large income *is* financial security. Nothing could be further from the truth, in these or any other times.

In some ways, the average family with an average income stands a better chance of becoming financially secure because it is easier to recognize the need to make financial security happen. In other words, a family making $15,000 a year is not lulled into thinking that financial well-being is derived from income alone. It isn't, whether that income is $15,000 or ten times that amount. The family with a large income may be in a better position to become financially secure, but it is no guarantee that it will happen.

The obvious conclusion to this dilemma serves as the basis for this book: *financial security does not necessarily mean making more money . . . but learning how to manage, save, invest, and protect the money you make.* Regardless of your present family or financial situation, financial security to an extent never dreamed possible (or perhaps only dreamed possible?) is within your reach. That reach must begin with the recognition that financial security does not just happen. You must make it happen. This book will help you achieve that goal, and in a much shorter period of time than you might imagine.

The first step toward your goal begins with a carefully prepared financial plan based on sound money management principles. In Section One, you will learn how to prepare and follow a financial plan designed to meet the needs of your family, not some hypothetical one. In order for a financial plan to work, it must be based on realistic family goals. Goals are incentives that encourage action in certain ways. This section shows you how to formulate and use goals that will make your financial plan work. You will also learn how to prepare a net worth statement and how it should be used in evaluating financial progress.

There is absolutely no substitute for financial planning in today's highly complex society. If you truly want a financially secure tomorrow for yourself and your family, you must devise a game plan leading to that goal. Section One gives you the framework for designing such a plan and shows you how to proceed, step-by-step.

Building for tomorrow must start today.

Nothing is more important in establishing financial security than learning how to save. A consistent savings program provides the foundation upon which investments can be safely laid. As you will learn in Section Two, many families either don't save at all (inconsistent saving falls into this category) or they save incorrectly (buying mutual funds or investing in the stock market before establishing a sound savings foundation). In addition to learning how to establish and nurture a consistent savings program, you will learn how much to save, how often to save, where to save, . . . and how to save even if you are in financial hot water. Above all else, you will learn this: *you cannot afford not to save, regardless of your present financial situation.*

In Section Three you will learn about the world of investments — from real estate to REITs, from stocks to bonds, from paintings to oil and gas leases on public lands. It is no secret that carefully chosen investments lead to financial wealth, and, as you will quickly learn, investing (as opposed to saving) is not reserved solely for families with first class incomes. Beginning with a consideration of inflation and its effect on the investment dollar, you will learn the rudiments and language of investing. You will also learn how to choose an investment medium that best suits your particular situation and needs. Specific guidelines for investing in various investment mediums are also presented in step-by-step fashion. Since the primary purpose of investing in the first place is to gain a greater return on funds than you could get from savings, emphasis is placed on conservative, informed money management principles, regardless of the investment medium chosen, to better insure your prospects for success. Such an approach promotes investment success, but nothing on earth can guarantee it.

The final Section of this book is in many ways the most important. Insurance brings together all the loose ends of an otherwise substantive family financial plan by guaranteeing that a set-upon financial program will not be interrupted when illness, accident, or worse occurs. This section covers the basic principles of and reasons for health insurance, life insurance, automobile insurance, and homeowner's insurance . . . including guidelines for evaluating your present coverage and

13

buying additional or replacement coverage. The special chapter on Medicare and Medicare supplement insurance will help you evaluate your Medicare insurance program or the program of a parent or grandparent. You will learn that mail order insurance can be a good buy under the right circumstances, and that some form of national health insurance appears to be just around the corner. The most important thing you will learn is how to protect your family's financial future effectively, efficiently, and informatively.

It is entirely possible for the family with less than a first class income to achieve first class financial security. Not only is it possible, *it is fundamentally necessary* in our inflation-prone world where, as the philosopher Heraclitus said, "Nothing is constant but change." To help you study and apply the information contained in this book, consider if you will (and commit to memory) the ageless wisdom of this ancient Chinese proverb:

The plans are man's, the odds are God's.

The proverb, you must agree, speaks for itself.

Do-It-Yourself Family Money Kit presents a four-part plan for your financial growth and prosperity. If you use it wisely, if you put all the parts together correctly, you *will* gain the most precious and desirable of all earthly treasures — *financial security.*

This book will show you how.

SECTION ONE

FAMILY FINANCES

A carefully prepared and faithfully followed financial plan is the framework of financial security.

CHAPTER TWO

GETTING YOUR FINANCES IN ORDER

THEY REALLY HAD IT MADE

John and Kathy really had it made. At least they thought they did. After all, both had good-paying jobs which, after taxes, brought slightly more than $30,000 per year into their three-year old household. Their life emphasis, if it can be so called, was to do and have everything that six years of college and graduate school postponed but made possible. Their pursuit was so oriented and all was Camelot.

But on the advent of their fourth year of marriage, the bubble burst and Camelot vanished before their eyes. While driving to work one wintry morning, John lost control of his car on an icy downhill stretch of road and the resulting accident left him paralyzed for life from the waist down. Most, but not all, of John's medical expenses were paid for by group insurance coverage, but his employer provided no salary continuance insurance to meet continuing income needs. Kathy, in taking a three-month leave of absence to care for John, had no continuing income whatsoever. And, because John required the services of a part-time nurse once Kathy was able to return to work, their household income after expenses was barely enough to make ends meet.

The real tragedy in this case is one shared needlessly by millions of families every year. They had never discussed, much less developed, a financial plan that could have virtually guaranteed for them a secure financial future. Their "live and spend for today" journey lasted three short years. It led to no savings, no additional insurance, and no hope of restoring the financial position they once enjoyed.

The purpose of this chapter is to help you develop and follow a financial plan guaranteeing that what happened to John and Kathy *never happens to you*. The method of financial planning discussed in this chapter — and which serves as the basis for other sections of this book — is presented in an easy-to-follow, easy-to-use format that lends itself to understanding and application by every family interested in real financial security. The very fact that you are reading this book reflects the motivation necessary to reach that goal. Coupled with the determination to succeed, you will achieve it.

A FINANCIAL PLAN IS NOT A BUDGET

Financial planning is an active process which should not be confused with budgeting, a passive process. In budgeting, the emphasis is on *stretching* financial resources to meet predetermined expense needs over which the budgeter exercises little if any control. There are predetermined expense needs in financial planning, but the emphasis is on *active, determinant* control over the way financial resources are managed. Budgeting suggests specific limitations in every aspect of spending, limitations that many families disavow as useless at the first sign of budgetary failure. Financial planning, on the other hand, promotes financial freedom within specific spending categories because two of the most important objectives of money management are actively planned for and pursued: (1) improving the family financial position through savings, investments and insurance, and of equal importance, (2) coping with and hedging against the effects of inflation.

Budgeting simply does not work for most families whereas a good financial plan, conscientiously developed and faithfully followed, will lead to financial security never dreamed possible.

PLAN AHEAD AND MOVE AHEAD

There is absolutely no substitute for financial planning in today's highly complex society. *The family that plans ahead moves ahead.* The family that doesn't usually has trouble maintaining the status quo and oftentimes falls behind. Both are undesirable. When tragedy strikes as it did for John and Kathy, it can be disasterous. If you will apply the principles of financial planning as discussed in this chapter, you will find yourself moving ahead, perhaps dramatically. It won't happen overnight, especially if you are one of the many who constantly falls behind. It is certainly no exception in financial planning that anything of lasting value requires lasting effort.

The fundamental purpose of preparing and following a financial plan is to help you manage income and expenses and to ultimately increase net worth. Stated another way, a financial plan will help you manage money in such a way that will result in increasing net worth (and beating inflation). It doesn't make any difference whether you are making $10,000 or $100,000 a year, a financial plan will enhance your financial position over a predictable period of time.

Financial planning will also enable you to overcome the fallacious belief that it takes a lot of money to make money. This may be true on a large scale, but not as far as the average family is concerned. Some of the soundest corporations in this country, financially speaking, are small ones that thrive in the shadows of the IBM's and Xerox's. Their strength lies in the fact that they manage income and assets carefully, watch expenses, and are satisfied with moderate growth. There is no reason why you can't enjoy similar success using similar measures.

If it's needed later, plan for it today.

If you have never attempted family financial planning before, some of the revelations of this chapter may surprise you. You're going to take a hard, calculated look at your income and its sources. You're going to review your expenses. For many, you will literally learn for the first time where your money goes. Most importantly, at least as far as your future is concerned, you're going to evaluate and in many cases formulate future goals. No amount of financial planning can be successful if you don't visualize, even dramatize, where the plan leads. We live in a goal-oriented society — short-range goals, intermediate-range goals, and long-range goals. Used properly, goals make things happen. Perhaps more correctly, goals provide the incentives necessary for us to act in such a way to make things happen

Keep this fact in mind as you study and apply the principles learned in this chapter: *financial stability and growth are attainable by anyone, regardless of income level.* The secret to becoming financially secure is in learning to manage money successfully. It is a step-by-step process that must begin with the conviction that you can do it and following through with those measures (actions, choices) that have led others to success.

THE FINANCIAL WORKSHEET: WHERE YOU ARE NOW

The first step in preparing a working financial plan is to establish a planning period. The 12-month calendar year is the most commonly used period, and is used for illustrative purposes here. However, any period will work if it fits your particular circumstances.

The next step is the most important — projecting income and expenses that are likely to occur during your planning period . . . *based on family goals.* This can be a trying step for many families, because it first requires a review of prior income and expense figures. Old tax forms, checkbook registers, receipts, and bank statements will have to be gleaned in order to make your projection as accurate as possible.

Using a worksheet format as exemplified in Figure 2-01 (the worksheet and other forms are replicated in the Appendix of this book), record the total net (disposable) income from all sources you received during the prior year (or other time span equal to the planning period chosen). *Don't overlook anything.* Wages, commissions, social security benefits, pensions, interest income, allowances, everything that represented disposable income for family use should be included.

When you are confident that your income calculation is correct, review all expenses that occurred during the same period. Again, don't omit any items. Check and re-check your records carefully to make sure your expense data is correct. Record your findings on a worksheet under appropriate categories as shown.

The purpose of the worksheet is to show how income has been used to satisfy family needs in the past, *before* you began financial planning. Don't be discouraged if your chart reveals some questionable spending habits. *It's supposed to.* If it doesn't, you probably overlooked something. Many families will even find expenses in excess of income. The important thing at this point is to have *all* income and expense data honestly and accurately recorded on your worksheet. When this has been accomplished, you are ready to make an evaluation of family goals as they relate to your spending habits.

FAMILY GOALS AND YOUR
FINANCIAL PLAN

You have now chosen a planning period to fit your circumstances and prepared a financial worksheet showing past income and expense data. This data will be used to project income and expenses *most likely* to occur during your planning period, so be certain your figures are as accurate as possible.

A word of caution: financial data as you have recorded on your worksheet becomes a *budget* for many families who reason, "it's worked for us in the past, it'll work for us in the future." The problem with this approach is that it's passive. It does not manifest active, determinant control over finances,

FIGURE 2-01: FINANCIAL WORKSHEET. Use this chart format to record income and expense data for the prior year (or other period of equal duration to planning period chosen). Be as accurate as possible. Omit nothing. Your figures will be used to project income and expenses most likely to occur during your planning period.

INCOME

	ANNUAL*	Monthly
TAKE-HOME INCOME, all sources	$_____	$_____
INCOME from interest, dividends, etc.	_____	_____
OTHER INCOME	_____	_____
TOTAL	$_____	$_____

EXPENSES

	Annual*	Monthly
FIXED EXPENSES		
Taxes not withheld from Income	$ _____	$_____
Money saved	_____	_____
Money invested	_____	_____
Insurance premiums _____	_____	_____
(Types of coverage) _____	_____	_____
_____	_____	_____
Mortgage or rent	_____	_____
Loan payments	_____	_____
Other credit payments	_____	_____
TOTAL FIXED EXPENSES:	$_____	$_____
VARIABLE EXPENSES		
Food and beverages	$_____	$_____
Utilities: Gas or oil	_____	_____
Electricity	_____	_____
Telephone	_____	_____
Water and sewer	_____	_____
Household operation and maintenance	_____	_____
Transportation: Automobile expenses	_____	_____
Public transportation	_____	_____
Clothing	_____	_____
Medical care	_____	_____
Dental care	_____	_____
Gifts and contributions (charity)	_____	_____
Educational expenses	_____	_____
Personal expenses	_____	_____
Special expenses	_____	_____
Miscellaneous expenses	_____	_____
TOTAL VARIABLE EXPENSES:	$_____	$_____
TOTAL EXPENSES, Fixed and Variable:	$ _____	$_____

*Other period if different from annual

22

control that is fundamentally necessary if you intend to guarantee improvement in your family's financial position. Your intention should be to *manage income and expenses, not let them manage you.* If you call the shots, if you determine what goals are important to your family and make spending choices based on those goals, then a significant degree of financial security is already on your side of the court. How financially well-off you become depends on how well you develop money management skills. Unquestionably, the process begins with a financial plan based on realistic family goals.

Every family has goals that serve as incentives to influence spending habits. The problem for most families is that they do not use realistic goals as incentives for planned money management practices. For example, buying a new $12,000 station wagon when a $7,000 hatchback would adequately satisfy the family need to carry the lawn mower back and forth between mother's house is not an efficient use of financial resources. It doesn't matter that you can afford the larger car. The point is that it is not really *needed* and, in this example, *is not a realistic solution to a necessary goal.*

Gaining an understanding of goals and how they influence money management habits is necessary if you are to prepare a workable financial plan. Such an understanding will help you evaluate past money management practices (from your worksheet), and suggest positive steps to change those practices where necessary.

Based on their expected achievement (target) dates, goals can be categorized as shown in Figure 2-02. Examples are also presented by category of what may be realistic goals for many families.

Simply stated, *goals make things happen.* Realistic goals make planned things happen. Carried one important step further, *stated goals* based on realistic *and reasonable* family wants and needs provide positive incentives for planned money management practices to achieve those goals.

What are your goals in life right now? What do you really want for yourself, for your family . . . within the next year, several years from now, ten years from now? These are important considerations that should be discussed with all family members old enough to contribute to the discussion.

Be realistic and reasonable about family goals: realistic in the sense that you would not expect to own a million dollar yacht on a $15,000 income; reasonable in the sense that what you want and strive for meets a realistic family need as efficiently as possible. You will also have to set priorities with respect to your goals so that money is used effectively and your plans reflect current family values.

Now, without referring to your worksheet, write down the goals that are important to you and your family. Follow the format shown in Figure 2-03 to *state* your goals. Assign a target date for achieving each listed goal, an estimated dollar cost value (what it will cost), and calculate the amount of money that would have to be saved monthly in order to buy the item outright on the target date. The following example is illustrative:

	GOAL	TARGET DATE	APPROX. COST	COST/MO.
Short-Range Goals	Emergency Fund	12 mos.	$ 600	$50
	Patio Furniture	12 mos.	168	14
Intermediate-Range Goals	Washer-Dryer	24 mos.	528	22
	New Television	24 mos.	432	18
Long-Range Goals	Boat-Trailer	60 mos.	5,400	90
	College Expenses	120 mos.	9,600	80

FIGURE 2-02. Although this is an oversimplified example which does not consider interest on savings or effects of inflation, it shows that a total of $274 must be put away for an initial period of 12 months, $210 per month for the next 12 months, $170 per month for the next 36 months, and $80 per month for the remaining 60 months in order to have cash for the goal items on the respective target dates.

You now have a written summary of what is important to you and your family, and an estimation of what these important goals are going to cost. Together with your completed worksheet, you are ready to prepare your financial plan.

FIGURE 2-03: IMPORTANT FAMILY FINANCIAL GOALS. Realistic and reasonable family goals, and your plan for financial achievement of each, should be recorded on a chart similar to the one below.

YOUR GOALS	TARGET DATE	APPROXIMATE DOLLAR VALUE	COST/MO.
SHORT-RANGE GOALS			
INTERMEDIATE-RANGE GOALS			
LONG-RANGE GOALS			

YOUR FINANIAL PLAN:
WHERE YOU'RE GOING

In order to prepare an effective, workable financial plan, you will now compare *every single item* on your completed worksheet with stated family goals. Once this step-by-step comparison of *past* money management practices to *current* family goals has been completed, your projection of *future* income and expenses onto a financial plan chart as shown in Figure 2-04 will be easy.

Notice that the worksheet and financial plan charts are subdivided into three distinct areas: *Income, Fixed Expenses,* and *Variable Expenses.* For each item shown under these subdivisions, ask yourself the following questions with respect to past money management practices:

1. Were they consistent with my family's important goals?

2. Were they effective and efficient in moving toward those goals?

If the data recorded on your worksheet shows that you have been practicing principles of money management that are meeting important family needs in an effective and efficient manner, your financial plan projections will probably parallel worksheet data. For most of us, however, *this won't be the case* and areas for definitive change beg for recognition. The following suggestions and pointers will help you recognize the not-so-obvious areas where change may be in order, and offer some guidelines to help you project income and expenses from your worksheet onto your financial plan chart.

Income: This is probably the most overlooked area when reviewing income and expense data because of the assumption "I'm stuck with what I make." However, this assumption does not necessarily hold true. For example, if you have been consistently receiving a large income tax refund every year, you may be having too much money withheld from your paycheck. Since the government does not pay interest on the money refunded, you may be ahead by changing your withholding status with your employer. In addition to receiving more in-

FIGURE 2-04: FINANCIAL PLAN. Use this chart format to record income and expenses most likely to occur during your planning period. Base projections on worksheet data evaluated against realistic and reasonable family goals, past money management practices, and your commitment to effectively and efficiently use family resources.

PROJECTED INCOME

	Annual*	Monthly
TAKE-HOME INCOME, all sources	$_____	$_____
INCOME from interest, dividends, etc.	_____	_____
OTHER INCOME	_____	_____
TOTAL	$_____	$_____

PROJECTED EXPENSES

	Annual*	Monthly
FIXED EXPENSES		
Taxes not withheld from Income	$_____	$_____
Financial Security: Savings	_____	_____
Investments	_____	_____
Life Insurance	_____	_____
Health Insurance	_____	_____
Automobile Insurance	_____	_____
Homeowner/apartment Insur.	_____	_____
Mortgage or rent	_____	_____
Loan payments	_____	_____
Other credit payments	_____	_____
TOTAL FIXED EXPENSES:	$_____	$_____
VARIABLE EXPENSES		
Food and beverages	$_____	$_____
Utilities: Gas or oil	_____	_____
Electricity	_____	_____
Telephone	_____	_____
Water and sewer	_____	_____
Household operation and maintenance	_____	_____
Transportation: Automobile expenses	_____	_____
Public transportation	_____	_____
Clothing	_____	_____
Medical care	_____	_____
Dental care	_____	_____
Gifts and contributions (charity)	_____	_____
Educational expenses	_____	_____
Personal expenses	_____	_____
Special expenses	_____	_____
Miscellaneous expenses	_____	_____
TOTAL VARIABLE EXPENSES:	$_____	$_____
TOTAL EXPENSES, Fixed and Variable:	$_____	$_____

*Other planning period if different from annual

come up front that won't be reduced prematurely by inflation, the additional income could be used to beef up a floundering savings program thereby increasing interest earnings. You may also be getting shortchanged on interest earnings from savings. The next Section is devoted entirely to savings and will provide some clues to help you get the most from your savings dollars.

When you have carefully evaluated past income data and made all the changes called for, record your projections onto your financial plan chart under similar headings. Don't forget to increase your take-home income estimate during the planning period by an amount equal to any increase *most likely* to occur during the period (dividends, cost-of-living raise, merit increase, etc.).

Being stuck with what you make is not a hard-and-fast rule as the discussion above suggests. Don't begin an evaluation of expenses until you have made every available adjustment and your income figure is correct.

Fixed Expenses: These are expenses over which you have little immediate control with respect to the amount that must be regularly paid. Mortgage or rent payments, automobile loan payments, insurance premiums and, in some cases utility payments on a budget plan are normally fixed expenses. Although you may not have *immediate* control over your fixed expense obligations, your answers to the two questions posed earlier may reveal inconsistencies with family goals and areas for definite change.

For example, a family making monthly payments on a $12,000 station wagon when a $7,000 hatchback would more realistically and reasonably meet the family need is not an effective or efficient use of resources. Nor are the following examples of fixed expenses that many families find themselves saddled with:

1. Payments on quasi-developed or undeveloped land in some far away paradise-in-the-making. Too often such fixed expenses are a waste of resources because the return on investment falls short of expectations. More on this in Section Three.

2. Insurance premiums for unnecessary insurance. Many families find themselves paying for insurance they don't need. If coverage under group insurance is 100%, *it is probably unwise* to spend money for additional insurance coverage. More on this in Section Four.

3. Excess use of credit. Interest charges on many credit card purchases could be avoided if current purchases are paid for when billed and big ticket items are planned and saved for. Avoid getting trapped by the lure of a tempting credit line and live-for-today-only thinking.

4. Investing before saving. Too many families find themselves sending monthly *investments* to mutual fund or similar companies before they have established any kind of savings program. Such investments are not savings and should never be started until a solid, consistent savings program has been set up. More on this in Section Two.

5. Mortgage or rent payments beyond means. This is the basis for many financial problems, especially for younger families who take on large house payments justified by two incomes. When one income stops, fixed and variable expenses become unmanageable.

As suggested above, the succeeding Sections of this book will influence your evaluation of fixed expense obligations in the areas of savings (obligation to pay yourself), investments, and insurance. These obligations are shown on the financial plan chart under the subheading "Financial Security" because together with your financial plan, they comprise the basis for current financial stability and future financial growth.

However, before reading further, you should at least make a *tentative projection* of fixed expenses you think are most likely to occur during your planning period. Let stated family goals guide your evaluation of worksheet data. Your projections, for the moment at least, must serve to reflect *im-*

mediate fixed expenses most of which can't be changed overnight.

Variable Expenses: These are expenses over which you have the greatest control because of their flexibility. Certain fixed and variable expenses may belong in the opposite category depending on family values and practices. For example, many families regularly contribute a fixed amount each week to their church or synagogue. This expense, then, should be moved to the fixed expense category.

Projecting variable expenses most likely to occur during your planning period will be easier if you keep in mind the fact that they are flexible. You *can* do something immediately to change money management practices that are not, as revealed on your worksheet, consistent with stated family goals. You *can* rearrange priorities and delay certain flexible expense items, or avoid some altogether. You *can* and you will recognize spending habits attributable to haphazard, impulse shopping sprees that really serve no purpose in your family's value system. Coming home with a bargain is a waste of family resources if it satisfies no real family need.

The following suggestions for reducing (in some cases eliminating) variable expense spending will help you complete your financial plan projections:

1. Eliminate unnecessary expenses altogether. For example, spending $84 for season concert tickets and attending four of eight performances is an ineffective and inefficient use of resources. It's also a classic example of poor money management.

2. Spend less for certain items. Take advantage of weekend specials, shop only from a list, avoid "convenience" items, stock up when items are in season. Above all, *buy an item only because you want it*, not because it happens to be the bargain of the day.

3. Make use of your own skills instead of paying for services. Hanging wallpaper in the master bedroom may not be your ideal weekend pastime, but it could save hundreds of dollars.

4. Use public transportation or carpool. Riding the bus to work just one day a week could shave 10-15% off your automobile expenses.

5. Take advantage of free community services for education and recreation (concerts, parks, libraries, art exhibits, lectures at nearby schools and colleges, local tennis courts, softball leagues, etc.).

6. Institute a "think it over" period for proposed variable expenses. You can avoid the "why did I ever buy that?" syndrome by simply using a think-it-over period for all major purchases, and many minor ones as well.

As you complete your financial plan record, keep in mind that family spending habits vary widely, within as well as between families. No family is immune to overspending and poor money management habits from time to time. The difference between families that move ahead financially and those that don't is the former's ability to recognize these habits before they get out of hand and take positive steps to correct them.

You have now completed a very positive step toward a secure financial future — laying out your financial plan. It is now time to learn how to put your plan to work effectively to guarantee financial growth and security.

PUTTING YOUR FINANCIAL PLAN TO WORK

The solution to money problems is not necessarily more money. Sometimes it is *learning how to get more* with the money you have, plus the patience and self-discipline to accomplish it. When this solution is understood and practiced, money problems become manageable and financial growth follows.

Your financial plan is a money management plan. It is characteristically unique to your family because it is based on your family's goals and dreams. This characteristic — *your* goals, *your* dreams — sets the plan far above a passive budget and makes it truly *workable* for your family situation.

31

Putting your plan to work means exercising active, positive control over financial resources and how they are used. It means making hard decisions about how money is spent and setting priorities for planned spending; it also means having — *and using* — the conviction and willpower to follow it through. Perhaps above all, it means learning how to make reasonable and realistic money choices based on what is important to you and your family.

The succeeding Sections of this book will greatly influence those choices. If you are not saving consistently to meet future planned (and unplanned) expenses, you will learn how to begin a sound savings program regardless of income level. You will also learn how to make future investment choices oriented to your family goals and how to insure your family and possessions properly and efficiently.

Managing income and expenses effectively and efficiently will perhaps be the greatest challenge facing the family in the years ahead. Your financial plan provides the framework to meet that challenge head on, and come out ahead. There is no better financial tool available to the family to guarantee financial stability and financial growth.

THE ANNUAL FINANCIAL CHECKUP

Every family should perform a regular financial checkup in the form of a *net worth statement*. Such a record provides a good overall picture of finances and can be prepared in an hour or less. When done on an annual basis, it shows at a glance whether you are getting ahead financially or falling behind and, in either case, how fast.

An accurate net worth statement can serve as a point of departure for the year ahead. If you are not making as much progress as you had expected, you can decide whether to stay on course or change your financial plan (spending and saving habits, family goals, priorities) for the coming year or other planning period.

FIGURE 2-05: NET WORTH STATEMENT

Net Worth Satement

Year: _____

ASSETS

Cash: amount on hand	$_____
savings accounts	_____
checking accounts	_____
House, current market value	_____
Other real estate, market value	_____
Household furnishings, value	_____
Automobile, current retail value	_____
Life insurance, cash value	_____
Stocks and bonds, current value	_____
Money owed you	_____
Other assets	_____
TOTAL	$_____

LIABILITIES

Mortgages, balance due today	$_____
Installment debts, balance due	_____
Credit card purchases, balance due	_____
Charge accounts, current balance	_____
Other debts, total amount owed	_____
TOTAL	$_____

NET WORTH

Assets minus liabilities	$_____

A net worth statement is simply a listing of assets and liabilities. Net worth is the difference between the two. Ideally, net worth will show positive growth each year and the minus side (liabilities) will get smaller. There may be good reasons why you'll fall behind sometimes, such as when you buy a new home or when other expenses are heavier than usual. If you are exercising positive control over your financial plan, however, your *cumulative* net worth will always reflect financial growth.

Use the net worth statement format shown in Figure 2-05 to determine present net worth. Compute net worth again on or about January 1st each year thereafter (or at the end of your planning period if it's not based on the calendar year). The figures will help you assess your progress.

ASSESSING YOUR OVERALL PROGRESS

Inflation plays havoc with any financial plan, but it wields disaster upon those who fail to formulate and follow one. You obviously want to create a financially secure future for yourself and the ones you love, and formulating and following a financial plan based upon realistic family goals will put you well on the road to accomplishing it. But in order to make sure that you are heading in the right direction at the fastest possible pace, you must objectively assess your progress on a periodic basis.

Set aside a *specific* time at the end of each planning period to evaluate your progress. Compare what you spent with what you planned to spend. If your spending was quite different from your plan, find out why. Your specific answer to the question "why?" should suggest ways to improve your next plan.

Don't rely entirely on the bottom line of your net worth statement to reflect financial progress. It provides a good overall picture, but it doesn't nor is it intended to show specific areas that might need improvement. The more efficient you become at managing income and expenses, the more funds you will have to divert into savings, investments . . . *financial security.*

Keep in mind that a financial plan is something you keep working at until it fits your family's needs. There is no perfect plan, there can be no perfect plan, because circumstances upon which it is based are constantly changing. Even though you might be satisfied with your financial plan as reflected by your financial progress today, it will need to be changed from time to time in order to satisfy your financial dreams of tomorrow. As circumstances change, reevaluate and reorganize your financial plan around new goals, needs, and wants.

Practice the principles of financial planning you learned in this chapter. There is no better way to guarantee financial growth and a secure future for yourself and, more importantly, the ones you love.

A path leading out of the woods must be followed in the right direction.

CHAPTER THREE

FINANCIAL COUNSELING

IS FINANCIAL COUNSELING NECESSARY?

Mike and Donna were in financial trouble. For several years, they had been making payments on two new automobiles, a new house, and a small vacation home which pushed their two incomes over the limit. Their family lifestyle and spending habits left barely enough resources to handle basic family expenses and no funds for savings. They were living from one paycheck to the next and, especially in recent months, spending more than they were bringing in.

Fortunately for this young family, they realized that a change had to be made, and soon. According to Donna, "We decided that the only way we were going to get out from under the gun was to prepare a financial plan and stick to it. Our spending habits had deteriorated to the point where we seemed to spend just for the sake of spending. We had no real savings and no real plans for the future. We just never came to grips with where we were going financially."

Within two weeks, Mike and Donna had drawn up a basic financial plan based on what they determined to be reasonable and realistic goals that they committed to writing.

However, their resulting financial plan was still unworkable: after trimming variable expense spending to conservative limits, their fixed expense obligations were such that total planned expenses continued to exceed planned, anticipated income.

They found a solution to their problem through a counselor for the *Consumer Credit Counseling Service* office in their community. Arrangements were made with two creditors to stretch out remaining car payments thereby reducing their monthly payment load. As the figures below indicate, they were able to reduce their fixed expense obligations and had funds left over for savings. Payments on their two houses were not interrupted and, as Donna put it, "We knew for the first time in our married lives where we were going financially and how we were going to get there."

CREDITOR	BALANCE	PAYMENT BEFORE	PAYMENT AFTER
Car #1	$3,848	$202	$136
Car #2	2,214	165	114

The counseling service that helped Mike and Donna solve their financial problem is available in most metropolitan communities across the country. The Consumer Credit Counseling Service offers basic financial, credit, and debt management counseling free for the asking, except for a nominal "paper work" fee (usually less than $10) that is often waived for families in serious financial trouble.

If your analysis of worksheet data (previous money management practices) and family goals (what is financially important to your family) results in a financial plan that either *can't* work because of serious money troubles or *won't* work to meet family expectations, by all means contact the Consumer Credit Counseling Service. You do not have to be in financial trouble to qualify for counseling, but you must be honest and straightforward with your counselor in seeking assistance. You will be expected to provide financial data similar to that recorded on your worksheet (it's kept confidential), and a complete review of family goals and priorities will be made. And, for families deeply in debt, credit cards will be destroyed and the assumption of additional debt will be discouraged until finances are again manageable. The location of the nearest office of the Con-

38

sumer Credit Counseling Service can be found in the white pages of your telephone directory.

Many family banking centers also offer free credit management counseling. If an office of the Consumer Credit Counseling Service is not located in or near your community, ask your local banker if credit management services are available through the bank. Banks are, in spite of *un*popular opinion to the contrary, *service* oriented industries. If you need financial guidance and have attempted to formulate a realistic financial plan, no conscientious banker would refuse your request for assistance whether or not formal family banking services are available, especially if your plan includes saving a portion of income on a regular basis.

Other than "paper work" fees, you do not have to pay someone for financial advice. Competent advice and counseling free of charge are available today in practically every community in this country, through the Consumer Credit Counseling Service, family banking center, or some other counseling service that may be available in your area. And regardless of how far in debt you might be, a debt consolidation loan is *not* a wise financial move. Some widely advertised financial counseling services offer nothing more than this, so be wary. Reputable counselors will never recommend consolidating debts because it results in a larger one.

Financial difficulties left unchecked have a way of becoming serious financial problems, so seek help if you need it. You will have a pretty good idea where major problem areas exist from your worksheet data and evaluation of family financial goals. If you are unable to overcome a financial obstacle in laying out your plan, *seek help*. The solution to every financial problem may not be as simple as the one described above, but there is a solution. And that solution could be the beginning to the reality of your financial dreams.

If you are unable to locate counseling services on your own, write to the National Foundation for Consumer Credit, 1819 H Street N.W., Washington, D.C. 20006. They will gladly provide you with the name and address of a non-profit credit counseling agency in your area.

SECTION TWO

SAVINGS

If one chooses not to save today, there will be nothing to invest tomorrow.

CHAPTER FOUR

SETTING UP A SOUND
SAVINGS PROGRAM

TWO CASE HISTORIES

No Savings. Jim and Carol had combined incomes totalling $27,500. Federal and state taxes reduced this amount to $21,524, a disposable income figure well above average for a young couple in their mid-twenties having no children and living in a midwestern city of 250,000 population.

Mortgage payments on their three-year old house came to $324 per month. Other average monthly expenses from their worksheet (Figure 4-01) were as follows: insurance premiums, $80.50; food and beverages, $469.17; utilities, $175.75; household operation and maintenance, $52.50; transportation expenses, $206.67; clothing, $69.17; other variable expense items, $119.17. The balance of their disposable income, *plus an additional amount*, went entirely to repay credit card bills ranging from a $3.90 bottle of perfume to a $1,400 Disney World vacation trip. In two short years of marriage, Jim and Carol accumulated more than $5,000 in credit card debts spread between eleven different credit card issuers. And, as Jim added, "We didn't add a single dollar to a $150 savings account opened for us two years earlier as a 'financial starter' wedding gift from Carol's parents."

FIGURE 4-01: JIM & CAROL'S WORKSHEET. Their savings account balance at the beginning of the period shown — $167.00.

INCOME

	ANNUAL*	Monthly
TAKE-HOME INCOME, all sources	$	$
INCOME from interest, dividends, etc.		
OTHER INCOME		
TOTAL	$ *21,524*	$ *1,794*

EXPENSES

	Annual*	Monthly
FIXED EXPENSES		
Taxes not withheld from Income	$ —	$
Money saved	—	
Money invested	—	
Insurance premiums *House*	*402*	*33.50*
(Types of coverage) *Auto*	*320*	*26.67*
Hosp. Supp.	*244*	*20.33*
Mortgage or rent	*3,888*	*324.00*
Loan payments		
Other credit payments *(Credit Cards)*	*5,256*	*438.00*
TOTAL FIXED EXPENSES:	$ *10,110*	$ *842.50*
VARIABLE EXPENSES		
Food and beverages	$ *5,630*	$ *469.17*
Utilities: Gas or oil	*1,125*	*93.75*
Electricity	*540*	*45.00*
Telephone	*312*	*26.00*
Water and sewer	*132*	*11.00*
Household operation and maintenance	*630*	*52.50*
Transportation: Automobile expenses	*2,480*	*206.67*
Public transportation	—	
Clothing	*830*	*69.17*
Medical care	*75*	*6.25*
Dental care	*120*	*10.00*
Gifts and contributions (charity)	*395*	*32.92*
Educational expenses	—	
Personal expenses	*705*	*58.75*
Special expenses	—	
Miscellaneous expenses	*135*	*11.25*
TOTAL VARIABLE EXPENSES:	$ *13,109*	$ *1,092.43*
TOTAL EXPENSES, Fixed and Variable:	$ *23,219*	$ *1,934.93*

*Other period if different from annual

FIGURE 4-02: KEITH & JANET'S WORKSHEET. Their savings account balance at the beginning of the period shown — $685.00.

INCOME

	ANNUAL*	Monthly
TAKE-HOME INCOME, all sources	$_____	$_____
INCOME from interest, dividends, etc.	_____	_____
OTHER INCOME		
TOTAL	$ 17,400	$ 1,450

EXPENSES

	Annual*	Monthly
FIXED EXPENSES	$ —	$
Taxes not withheld from Income	456	38.00
Money saved	3,780	315.00
Money invested **(Growth Mutual Fund)**	318	26.50
Insurance premiums ___House___	285	23.75
(Types of coverage) ___Auto___	428	35.67
___Life___	2,520	210.00
Mortgage or rent	1,110	92.50
Loan payments	372	31.00
Other credit payments		
TOTAL FIXED EXPENSES:	$ 9,269	$ 772.42
VARIABLE EXPENSES		
Food and beverages	$ 4,896	$ 408.00
Utilities: Gas or oil	—	
Electricity	1,245	103.75
Telephone	204	17.00
Water and sewer	99	8.25
Household operation and maintenance	393	32.75
Transportation: Automobile expenses	648	54.00
Public transportation	—	
Clothing	118	9.83
Medical care	—	
Dental care	36	3.00
Gifts and contributions (charity)	195	16.25
Educational expenses	—	
Personal expenses	297	24.75
Special expenses	—	
Miscellaneous expenses		
TOTAL VARIABLE EXPENSES:	$ 8,131	$ 677.58
TOTAL EXPENSES, Fixed and Variable:	$ 17,400	$ 1,450.00

*Other period if different from annual

Obviously, Jim and Carol are not a typical family with credit card debts in excess of $5,000. However, they are typical of many families who *use credit excessively, spend more than they make,* and *don't save at all.* This combination of financial mistakes is more prevalent during periods of high inflation. But high inflation or not, these financial miscues lead to financial disaster.

Investing Before Saving. The financial worksheet of Keith and Janet (Figure 4-02) reflects yet another financial mistake prevalent among many families. It also demonstrates that living within an income is no assurance of future financial growth.

Their income after taxes came to $17,400. Mortgage payments on their ten-year old house came to $210. Other monthly expenses, including insurance premiums, loan and credit payments, food and beverages, and all remaining variable expenses, averaged $887. This left a hefty $353 per month — nearly 25% of disposable income — for savings and investments, a feat few families manage even with higher incomes. But herein begins their dilemma. Of this $353 amount, $315 was used to purchase shares in a mutual fund through a fund representative the year before. Not only was a considerable portion of their investment dollar going for the salesman's commission thereby reducing the actual investment amount by a significant percentage the first year, but the investment fund was growth-oriented meaning that the potential return on investment was credible on a long-range basis at best.

Keith and Janet's dilemma is basic: *investing without a supporting savings foundation is a risk no family should assume.* With a savings balance of only $685 at the beginning of the period, the $38 per month allocated to their savings program provides no substantive support to their set upon investment program.

The Two Extremes. The financial dilemma of these two families represents two extremes in our society — *those who don't save at all,* and *those who save incorrectly.* Saving in the manner of Keith and Janet is self-defeating. Their investment dollars are needed for shorter-range goals which their current savings can not adequately meet. More often than not, such an investment program is doomed from the start. Jim and Carol, in not saving at all, are in real financial trouble. Unless some changes are made, they will never enjoy the simple satisfaction of just making ends meet. They will certainly never experience the peace of mind that only money put aside can bring.

There is a *fundamental difference* between saving and investing. It must be understood clearly and adhered to relentlessly if you are to realistically determine and evaluate the necessary steps that will lead to financial security.

SAVINGS ARE NOT INVESTMENTS

Many families mistakenly confuse saving with investing. The terms are, of course, related in the financial goal sense, *but they are not the same.*

Savings represent a basis, a *foundation basis* upon which investments can be safely and consistently made. If the foundation is strong enough, it will support a carefully planned investment program. An inadequate savings foundation usually results in inconsistent investing, interrupted investing, or both.

Subsequent sections of this chapter will help you determine what constitutes an adequate savings foundation for your family and how that foundation can best be achieved.

SAVE FOR SHORT-RANGE NEEDS

The purpose of a good savings program is threefold: (1) to primarily meet *short-range*, anticipated monetary needs, (2) to provide a *resource* to handle emergencies, and (3) to provide a *foundation* or basis for future investments. In addition, until a good foundation for investments exists, savings will provide funds to meet intermediate- and long-range goals as well.

A basic savings program is within the reach of any family that truly desires the financial security that comes only from putting money away. Franklin Jones said, "When a man begins to think seriously of saving for a rainy day, it's usually a rainy day." Unfortunately, as in one case cited earlier, many families don't entertain such thoughts even in a downpour! This is a sad truism of our times, because savings promote a sense of independence and security for the family that cannot be achieved in any other way.

We all have anticipated goals that require money financing. And emergencies, though not classic goals, require anticipation and money financing. A well-planned savings program will provide the funding necessary to meet these contingencies, and at the same time promote that sense of well-being that Jim and Carol have never known and Keith and Janet only thought they knew. There is absolutely no substitute for saving in today's world, regardless of your present financial situation. This chapter will help you begin and manage a sound, growing savings program that will meet short-range goals and emergencies and that will, before you know it, serve as a basis for building an investment program.

THE SAVING HABIT

Never before in the history of our nation has the practice of thrift become so important a consideration as on the advent of the 21st century. As a nation, we must come to grips with the reality of our dwindling natural resources and the significant role each of us must play in conserving and saving that which cannot be replaced. And as individual family units, we must accept the omnipotent fact that any such effort, large or small, begins in the home.

Thrift must be practiced in order for it to become a habit. The process of saving — the foremost practice of thrift in the home — is fundamentally more important than the amount saved. Andrew Carnegie said, "The best way to accumulate money is to resolutely bank a fixed portion of your income, no matter how small the amount." The amount is unimportant because once a regular pattern of setting a certain amount aside in savings is accomplished, you will find yourself increasing that amount automatically and frequently. Once it becomes a habit, and it will if you persist, you will consider *paying yourself* one of the most rewarding experiences of your life.

There is an old adage that goes, "Pay yourself first and there will be plenty to go around." The practice of thrift from a savings standpoint leads to thrift in other areas of life. Those who do not save a portion of income generally do not practice thrift to any significant degree in other areas of family life as well.

PAY YOURSELF FIRST

It is not difficult to acquire the saving habit. Like any habit, practice is the key to achievement. But you must start toward that goal. And once you start, *don't stop.*

The average family spends about 70% of income for the essentials of life — food, clothing, shelter, and transportation — leaving about 30% of income to cover other expenses. Obviously, these percentages can and do vary from one family to another. However, savings should take priority, at least from the standpoint of beginning a savings program and making it become a habit in your life, in considering how to apportion available disposable income. This priority must also be established by families that never seem to have enough money to make ends meet, much less commit to savings.

If you do not already have a savings plan, the best way to begin is to literally adopt the maxim,

I will pay myself first.

Such an adoption does two things. It reflects a conviction that you want to save, and it creates an obligation to save as though the self-payment is a debt. Everyone identifies with the conviction to pay debts — mortgage payments, car payments, and so on. A debt *regularly paid to yourself*, however, will have as its reward the ultimate financial well-being that only savings (and subsequently investments) can bring. The maxim also applies to those who already have some savings put away, but who do not regularly add to it. Again, the amount added is unimportant at first. The act of saving on a regular basis perpetuates itself. It has been stated that although practice does not necessarily make perfect, *it makes consistent*. In the long run when saving is involved, consistency produces its own sweet rewards.

HOW OFTEN AND HOW MUCH TO SAVE

A portion of income should be added to a savings program *at least monthly*, the same way bills are paid. If income from work is paid more often, write a check to yourself and deposit it in savings after each pay period. A small amount added every two weeks, for example, to an interest-paying savings account will yield more than if you added twice that amount on a monthly basis, especially if the account pays interest daily or continuously. For all practical purposes, a monthly savings deposit made on or about the same date each month will produce efficient savings growth, and the check to yourself can be written at the same time your other debts are paid. Notice the statement "your other debts." You owe it to yourself and your family, it's an obligation, so write that check regularly and with conviction.

How much should you save? An idealistic suggestion is offered in the following chronicle:

> To determine how much should be saved, calculate the amount of money you will need to satisfy all of your short- and intermediate-range goals over the next four years. Increase that amount by 50% and divide by 48 (number of months in four years).

Such an idea has merit because it would, for most families, include funds needed for a new car, several vacations, house repairs, college expenses. Assuming the determination is made every year in January when all household expenses are being reviewed for tax purposes, the necessity to finance that new car, vacation, college expense, or anything else for that matter would be considerably reduced. You would have the necessary funds, plus interest, to satisfy your family's needs.

From a practical standpoint, and especially for families that have never developed a consistent saving habit, the best way to determine how much to save is to use the *"Net Income - 10% Rule."* It is effective because it is simple. And, if at all possible, it should be considered as the minimum amount with which to start your savings program. All you do is calculate 10% of your net (take-home) income and use this figure as the savings amount. For example, a family bringing home $1,000 per month should *try* to save at least $100 per month. If you can't start with 10%, start with what you can and gradually increase that amount. You may have to do some rearranging of priorities in your financial plan to start a successful savings program, but it will be worth it if it leads to development of the saving habit in your life. Many people make the mistake of trying to save too much too soon. When they can't keep up with this shotgun approach, they quit. Start out with what you can afford and make that savings deposit regularly.

Developing the habit of regular savings is so important in family life that *you cannot afford not to save.* Even if you are in financial trouble, living beyond your means and literally in financial hot water, you can still afford to save. If you find your money management practices out of control, seek competent advice. Here are two excellent sources for financial advice that can be found in most communities (also see chapter three):

Consumer Credit Counseling Service. One of the services provided by this agency is debt management. For a nominal fee (sometimes no fee at all), a counselor will help you set up a debt repayment schedule satisfactory to the parties involved. For families already in financial trouble, such debt management action could well be the beginning of a new financial future that includes a savings program.

Local Family Bank Advisor. Many banks offer financial counseling services through family banking departments. In addition to being good public relations for the bank, these services are an excellent source of help for the family. Even if your local bank has no separate family banking arrangement, competent advice is generally available especially if you are a steady bank customer. There are plenty of progressive, family-oriented banks today that offer free financial advisory services. If yours doesn't, it may pay you to bank at one that does.

Don't Pay For Advice. Other than the nominal "paper work" fee charged by the Consumer Credit Counseling Service or some family banking departments, you do *not* have to pay someone for debt counseling services and you shouldn't. Some credit counseling agencies whose services are advertised widely offer nothing more than a debt consolidation loan. The resulting single monthly payment may be attractive, but the period of repayment and high interest costs won't be.

It may not be possible for you to apply the *Net Income-10% Rule* in the early stages of your savings program, especially if your spending habits require an immediate overhaul. But developing the saving habit in your life is too important not to at least get started.

If you already have a savings account but have not consistently added to it, *resolve to pay yourself first* and make it a monthly commitment.

If you do not already have a savings account, you have more than enough reasons to start one and to resolutely bank a portion of income on a regular basis.

Regardless of the amount that you are able to start saving, determine to be consistent in your savings effort. You will find paying yourself first and on a regular basis one of the most satisfying experiences in your family's life. And you will also find rearranging priorities around your savings goal one of the most welcome challenges in your financial planning.

You and your family are the primary beneficiaries of these efforts. If you make these efforts foremost in your life, they will pay the rewards you expect and deserve.

WHERE TO SAVE

Your savings should be kept in a bank or other savings institution that meets the following criteria: (1) *Safety* — are you assured of getting back at least the same number of dollars that you deposit; (2) *Liquidity* — if funds must be taken out immediately, can you withdraw them with ease; and (3) *Convenience* — do you have convenient access to the place where savings are to be kept.

A fourth factor that should be considered is *Yield*. This is simply the amount of interest, including the manner in which it is calculated, that is paid for the use of your saved dollars.

There are basically four types of savings institutions that meet the criteria discussed above. Ranked according to the institution that pays the *highest* interest first, they are credit unions, savings and loan associations, mutual savings banks, and commercial banks. At the moment, the federal ceiling on commercial banks is 5¾%. Mutual savings banks and savings and loan associations have a ceiling of 6%. Banks paying more than these amounts cannot be federally insured, although they may be insured by various state agencies. Credit unions, if you have access to one (through your place of employment or in many cases through your church), can and usually yield higher interest rates on savings but could be less advantageous since their counseling and other financial services may be limited. In some cases, such unions may not be insured.

By all means select a savings institution that best fits *your* needs, even if it means sacrificing the highest possible yield that you can get. Yield is important, but unless you are dealing with large amounts from the start, the difference in yield between 5¾% and 6% is not important. It may *become* important later on, but not at first. An institution that serves you in all aspects of financial matters is worth every one of your savings dollars if differences in yield are slight.

Many banks offer free checking accounts to savers. If you maintain at least a minimum savings balance, checks are free. The money saved in check charges alone at a bank paying 5¾% would, in many instances, more than offset the difference in interest earned from a bank paying higher rates but offering no free checking account privileges.

Interest-bearing checking accounts are also available at many banks. Checking and savings are combined into a single account enabling continuous interest earnings on deposited funds. The one drawback is that these accounts generally stipulate a minimum balance or minimum *average* monthly balance below which charges are assessed. If you can't maintain the required minimum balance, stay with separate accounts.

Whatever you decide, don't choose a bank or other savings institution paying less than 5¾% or one that doesn't meet the first three criteria discussed above.

How interest is figured is also an important consideraton, especially if there are many competing banks in your community. All factors considered equal, you should choose an institution that computes interest continuously, simply because more frequent compounding increases yield. To better understand how compounding affects interest, consider the annual amount of interest payable on $1,000 at various frequencies of compounding at 5¾%:

NO COMPOUNDING AT ALL	$50.00
ANNUAL COMPOUNDING	57.50
SEMIANNUAL COMPOUNDING	58.33
QUARTERLY COMPOUNDING	58.75
DAILY COMPOUNDING	60.03
CONTINUOUS COMPOUNDING	60.04

The more often interest is paid to your account, the

greater your yield will be. More and more banks are programming their computers to compound continuously, so you should have no problem finding the right place for your money. And without going into any of the more than 50 ways that banks actually compute that interest, it is sufficient only to say that you should look for a bank that does its computations *from day-of-deposit to day-of-withdrawal.*

Many banks offer automated tellers where deposits and withdrawals may be made 24 hours a day, seven days a week. These highly sophisticated banking systems, called *electronic funds transfer systems (EFTS)*, are changing the definition of convenience for many depositors. If you like what they have to offer, seek them out. Many such banks allow transfer of funds between checking and savings accounts by a simple telephone call. Ultimately, EFTS is destined to replace checks altogether and it is already used in various locations for paying bills, buying goods and services, and so on. Banks are getting tired of the paperwork involved with checks, and computer technology is such that makes EFTS possible not just in large cities but in small towns and communities as well.

HIGHER RETURNS ON YOUR SAVINGS

It is possible to obtain even higher interest on your savings dollar, *but not without pitfalls.* Certificates of deposit (called CD's), or time deposits, do pay much higher interest rates, but you must be able to leave the funds untouched for the period of time required for maturity. Withdrawal of funds before maturity could result in loss of all or part of the lucrative interest rates, depending on the type of account you have.

This early withdrawal pitfall also applies to *six-month money market certificates* ($10,000 minimum purchase) and one-year *all-savers certificates* ($500 minimum purchase). There are other high interest-paying possibilities as well, some geared to the small saver and some not. They may be considered, but don't overlook the pitfalls inherently tied to them.

The best advice is to *approach with caution* these higher interest-paying mediums until you and saving are comfortable friends. If your savings program is sound and consistent already, then by all means consider the higher-yielding alternatives. You will know if your income and savings are sufficient to warrant purchasing the more profitable CD's, certificates or various risk-free government savings bonds. *Warning:* if the balance in your basic savings account is less than three times your net monthly pay and if during the past 12-month period that balance has been reduced through withdrawals by more than 50%, you are probably not ready to consider any alternative that results in a monetary penalty for early withdrawal of funds.

ESTABLISHING YOUR SAVINGS GOAL

Remember that the primary purpose of saving is to satisfy, without having to borrow, your short-range financial needs, and at the same time build a financial foundation upon which investments can be made. For families that do not possess the income means for true investments, savings can serve to meet long-range goals and provide an investment resource in later years.

Until recently, most financial experts advised establishing a minimum savings goal equal to about six months total net income. Such an amount would, for most families, provide an adequate emergency fund and funds for meeting predetermined monetary needs. Investing, as opposed to saving, could be properly considered after that amount was safely put away.

Such advice today is uncommon and unrealistic, primarily due to high inflation. When inflation rates were lower, regular savings account interest rates provided a means of conserving purchasing power, even increasing it slightly. But regular savings accounts can't keep pace with today's inflation, nor are they likely to in the future.

Savings accounts are fundamentally important, however. They provide a means of ready cash that families need plus a psychological buffer that only money put away can create. A more realistic minimum savings goal for most families is an amount equal to about three months net income. Once this amount is laid up, investments can and should be properly considered.

Many families will have to do an about-face in their spending habits in order to achieve the financial security and well-being that savings and later investments provide. Setting specific savings objectives and developing the saving habit will bring such rewards in a much shorter period of time than many people realize. Where would you be now, financially, if you had started a 10% savings program just twelve months ago?

It's unrealistic to believe that a savings account will ever again keep pace with inflation. But it's also unrealistic to believe that you can make sound investment decisions necessary to beat inflation without one. Savings accounts *are* that important, and they probably always will be.

SAVINGS vs. INFLATION

High inflation makes a strong case for spending rather than saving, mainly because costs of goods and services rise faster than the value of saved dollars. However, goods and services cannot take the place of a ready cash reserve or the psychological comfort that such a reserve imparts.

The simple truth is that *people must save.* It's the way we live and inflation doesn't change what one social scientist has described as "the innate necessity of mankind." That innate necessity if carried to fruition leads to financial well-being by first leading to a firm foundation for investing. Without that foundation, you will not be able to make the decisions necessary to invest wisely or consistently.

The next section of this book is about the world of investments. It is also about beating inflation and growing financially. Although it is possible to give inflation a good race by using some form of savings program, the degree of risk increases with the increase in rate of return. Until you have harbored away funds in a safe, liquid, and convenient savings program, *don't take those risks.* Work on establishing and achieving your minimum savings goal. When you reach it, when you and saving are comfortable friends, you're ready to consider investments. Until that time comes, . . .

Save. And don't let inflation talk you out of it.

Your future cannot help but begin today.

SECTION THREE

INVESTMENTS

Successful investing is simple. All you have to do is choose investments that will go up in value.

CHAPTER FIVE

THE WORLD OF INVESTMENTS

INTRODUCTION

The single greatest investment most people make in their lifetime is their home. With few exceptions, a home represents the best hedge against inflation that anyone could have. A home purchased wisely in a good location increases in value year after year, and on the average has outdistanced inflation. The key to such success lies in the fact that fixed dollars go into *most* home financing arrangements and as inflation reduces the purchase power of the dollar, those invested dollars increase dramatically. Appreciation also increases the value of a home investment, and the demand for developed real estate should continue to rise for years to come.

The average cost of a home in 1976 was about $46,000. That average figure stood at just over $80,000 in 1981, and it continues to rise. Inflation, which generally refers to increased prices brought on by an increase in buying power outstripping available goods, certainly contributes to such increases, and no one knows if or when it will subside.

Whether inflation can be brought under control would not affect the value of a home as far as its relative investment punch is concerned, simply because *the demand for homes has kept prices rising.* Many economists believe that a slight degree of inflation is desirable in our society because employment is generally assured for everyone and the standard of living steadily rises.

But economists and everyone else agrees that recent inflation levels are too high. For the prospective investor, this forecasts concern and the need for knowledgeable financial management. If you have reached the point in your savings program where the next logical step suggests the consideration of investments, you should first gain a working knowledge of what inflation is and how it affects you and the dollar you've got to invest.

INFLATION AND THE INVESTMENT DOLLAR

Inflation benefits those who have goods because the demand for those goods is usually high. Employment is generally higher to keep up with production demands, investments are up to finance production plants, and workers' salaries are generally higher because competition is keen. The emphasis during such times is on *spending* rather than *saving* and, under nonwartime conditions, the consumer's purchasing power continuously induces industry to turn out more goods.

This is a highly desirable situation up to a point, but economists and government leaders have not found a way to maintain a level of inflation that guarantees prosperity for everyone. Indeed, in our society today, there is no such level outside the realm of theoretical economics.

There are many good investment opportunities during even rampant inflationary times. An extreme example of this occurred in Germany after World War I when speculators amassed fortunes while people on fixed incomes of $6,000 a year could not even buy a loaf of bread. Since inflation can be induced artificially by an increase in the supply of bank credit or by a general loss of confidence in national currency, investments made in poorly chosen mediums can be disasterous.

Runaway inflation, without government intervention, can lead to *deflation*. Deflation is generally coincident with economic depression and is characterized by an overabundance of goods compared with the amount of money in circulation. Some economists believe that economic depression is a cyclical consequence of a society based on competition. Others believe that a mild economic slowdown (recession) is the basic result and necessity of the free enterprise system. The latter is a more reasonable conclusion because our nation remembers all too well the lessons of 1929. We are taking steps to balance payments with other nations and to eliminate or at least reduce deficit spending, both major causes of inflation. However, our nation is one of widespread, diverse interests. This suggests the frustrating conclusion that *there can be no simple solution to so complex a problem.*

Since the purpose of investing is to earn a greater return on invested dollars than can be expected from savings, your investment medium must be chosen *informatively*. Track record of the medium in inflationary times takes on greater importance, and the wise first-time investor should choose an investment medium that has, over the years, exhibited a tendancy to be less affected by economic downfalls. The emphasis is *less affected* because no medium escapes adverse economic conditions altogether. Track record of any investment medium is no guarantee of future results, but it is an indicator which deserves your utmost attention.

The best advice for the prospective investor is advice seasoned with conservatism and informative management. Double digit inflation for the long-term seems unlikely, but inflation around the 7% mark may become known as the *new normal*.

Prudent, informative management of your investment dollars during any economic period is, of course, desirable and necessary to obtain the best results. During periods of high inflation, careful investing backed by informative management is *a must* in order to effectively offset the inflated effect of the dollar from one year to the next.

To illustrate inflation's ability to reduce purchasing power, consider a fund of $2,000. A rate of 7% inflation will reduce the purchasing power of this fund to $1,860 after one year, to $1,730 after two years. You would need an average annual return on investment of about 7% just to stay even. What does this say for savings accounts yielding 5¾ to 6 percent? Before you condemn savings accounts entirely, *and you shouldn't*, consider the value of unsaved money from one year to the next.

You *can* beat inflation if you respect the fact that it is an integral part of today's life. The first step toward conserving and increasing the purchasing power of your dollar lies in understanding the effects of inflation. The second involves choosing an investment medium that will come as close as possible to guaranteeing growth of those invested dollars over and above the inflation rate.

It must be repeated: never use your minimum savings account funds for investment purposes, regardless of economic conditions that may exist. When you have saved an amount equal to about three months' net income, then any funds over that amount may be considered for investment purposes.

The following chapters of this section will help you select an investment medium that best suits your family's needs and goals. It will be no easy selection because there are probably as many ways to invest money as there are ways to spend it.

Remember, too, that *investment involves risk*, regardless of the medium chosen or the economic climate at hand. If you are willing to do a little homework, you can minimize the risk element considerably. Homework means gaining an understanding of the essential forces at play and applying common sense logic toward managing them. It does not take an economist to describe the effects of inflation any more than it takes a meteorologist to tell you when it's raining. That is the kind of common sense this section will help you use in choosing where to put those investment dollars.

YOUR INVESTMENT WORLD: EVALUATING GOALS

As has already been stated, investing in real estate has proven to be one of the most successful hedges against inflation around. For the long-term potential in general (and beating inflation in particular), investing in real estate in one's own community offers tremendous prospects for investment gain. More on this later.

The fundamental rule of investing is that *you shouldn't invest* (as opposed to save) *money that you can't afford to lose.* If you have decided that investing toward a financially secure future is for you, then you should define your investment goals in much the same way that you defined your savings goals.

Evaluate you investment goals in terms of *safety, liquidity,* and *convenience.* Sound familiar? It should, because the basic rules of saving apply to investing, inasmuch as possible depending on your specific goal objectives.

For example, if your primary investment goal is growth of capital which, for most people, it should be, then investing in stocks, real estate, art objects, and the like, though capable of meeting your goal objectives, will take on a slightly different definition of safety, liquidity, and convenience. The important thing to remember in evaluating your investment goals against these factors is that they become "relative" to the investment medium. It takes *time* to sell real estate, you may have trouble *finding a buyer* when you want to sell, the market may be *down* at that forced point.

As far as your personal investment objective is concerned, however, the degree to which these factors affect your investment decisions will influence your selection of an investment medium. If you aren't comfortable with a proposed investment medium because of any of these factors, seek another. Your goals will probably be fine, and there are many investment routes available to you.

INVESTMENT STRATEGY

Investment goals can best be achieved if your investment strategy includes an annual checkup of the following points: (1) *diversity of investments*, (2) *their flexibility*, and (3) *are the results beating inflation*.

Diversity simply means not keeping all your eggs in one basket. The best avenue of diversification for the small investor lies in mutual funds, and the professinal management of a well-chosen fund can pay off handsomely over the long term. The purpose of diversification is, of course, to increase your chance of gain by reducing your prospect of loss. If you own only stocks and a long *bear market* prevails (meaning stock prices are falling), you could lose more than if you had diversified your investments between, for example, stocks and bonds.

Flexibility means not becoming married to an investment medium. If the chosen medium is not producing the results you expected, find another. You certainly would not want to sell a corporate or government bond when the money market is yielding 10% or more, unless inflation was much higher. But you would switch that security if the going rate was half that amount. Or at least you would seriously consider such a move.

Results are results, and they are best measured against the inevitable major standard, the rate of inflation. If you're beating inflation, great. If not, go back one paragraph. If you are holding stocks, you can also gauge your results in relation to the market as a whole. A real estate investor should be able to equate his results in relation to the market trend in his area, assuming holdings are in the investor's community which they should be. The name of the game is results, measured in age old terms of gains and losses. If you confuse the two, investing is definitely not your game.

INVESTMENT OPPORTUNITIES ABOUND

The list of investment opportunities is practically endless. Such a list would include *real estate, real estate investment trusts (REITs), preferred and common stocks, convertibles, corporate bonds, government bonds, municipal bonds, mutual funds for growth, mutual funds for income, mutual funds for growth and income, old books, old films, inventions, oil and gas leases, prints, paintings, diamonds, stamps, gold, silver, options, futures, auction items* — the list goes on and on.

If you are an expert or quasi-expert in some area that has investment potential, by all means consider it as an investment medium. Familiarity can go a long way toward helping you attain your personal investment objectives. For example, let's assume you know a great deal about French paintings. Works by Etienne, a contemporary French painter, are selling for twice what they were three years ago (*almost true* by the way) and you have an opportunity to buy three such paintings under forced sale circumstances. You know art, you know (the reputation of) Etienne, you recognize the demand for his works is increasing rapidly, the available supply is limited — of course you'd buy them. If you know what you're doing and recognize the investment opportunity available, don't hesitate to take advantage of it. *A word of caution to the non-expert:* collectibles such as paintings, coins, stamps, prints, and the like are potentials for investment in the hands of those who know what they're doing. If you aren't well informed, stay away from them for investment purposes.

Tomorrow's reflection reveals todays past.

TAX SHELTERS FOR EVERYONE

If you are not covered by a federally-qualified *and successfully-invested* company pension plan, you should consider allocating a portion of your investments to a tax-deferred *Individual Retirement Account* (or *Keough Plan* for self-employed workers). Such a consideration would be wise even if your current pension arrangement is sound and on the right track.

An IRA is regarded by most experts as the simplest, safest and most lucrative means of assuring financial security during retirement years. Most of the investment mediums discussed in this Section — e.g., stocks, bonds, mutual funds *but not* precious metals, precious stones or collectibles — qualify for IRA *contributions* (investments), and an account may be set up almost anywhere — e.g., banks, savings and loans, brokerage houses or mutual fund managers.

Today's inflationary economy and Social Security's funding problems give added importance to an IRA and Keough *tax shelter*. All workers, whether covered by a company pension plan or not, may contribute up to 15% of income or $2,000 a year into an IRA (up to $4,000 for a working couple, up to $2,250 for a worker and non-working spouse; the Keough limit is $15,000). Taxes on interest, dividends and capital gains are deferred until funds are withdrawn during retirement years when the tax bite is (projected to be) smaller.

There is one serious drawback to IRA contributions. If it becomes necessary to withdraw funds from your account prior to age 59½, a sizeable interest penalty is assessed. The resulting conclusion demands emphasis: *don't allocate investments to an IRA that could be needed for short- or intermediate-range goals.* Your savings program and non-IRA investments should be set up and managed to meet your pre-retirement wants and needs *before* allocating IRA or Keough contributions.

You should also keep in mind that contributions to an IRA or Keough require the same "money management" considerations as your other investments. If they aren't faring as well as they should, money in your account can be shifted from one investment to another once a year without penalty, and as often as necessary if your account manager remains the same.

Fees charged for managing an IRA can range from nothing at many banks and no-load mutual funds to a substantial amount at brokerage houses managing an active stock portfolio. Be sure that you have a complete understanding — and acceptance — of the charges involved *before* starting your account.

An IRA or Keough Plan used properly will go a long way toward helping you achieve your important investment goals . . . and making those retirement years *the best possible years* of your life. You deserve no less.

CHAPTER SIX

REAL ESTATE, THE BEST HEDGE

AN OMAHA SUCCESS STORY

Carefully selected real estate is the best investment medium available today. This fact is especially true for the small investor as the following story illustrates.

In 1974, the land upon which the Haddon home is located was an undeveloped, wooded area adjacent to one of Omaha's wealthiest residential districts. Densely treed and attainable by only a single gravel road leading to one of the many small parks on Omaha's southwest side, the land went unnoticed for years, serving as a perfect boundary for the few homes that had been built toward the end of the two-block, secluded lane several years before.

On a Sunday afternoon of that year, Jeff and Pam Haddon *discovered* the small hideaway, to their amazement only minutes from interstate access to anything the city has to offer. Distances in Omaha aren't measured in miles. A good array of major streets and various interstate loops and circles reduce such measurements to the level of time. Pam first saw the small sign nailed to a tree, "Lot for Sale by

Owner — Phone 000-0000," but the proximity to that rich section of the city discouraged them, for the moment at least, from making a telephone inquiry. Inquiries the week before encouraged by similar signs in similar locations — they were programmed to envision similar asking prices around the $30,000 figure. "Let's not go through with that again" was their first abandon-the-high-hopes conclusion.

But they did make that phone call the following day, and if ever a lesson is to be learned in real estate transactions, *learn it from their experience.* The asking price was not $30,000, or $20,000, not even $10,000. It was $9,500! Their first reaction was there must be a mistake. Of course, the reaction was shared with one another, not with the voice on the phone agreeing to meet them at the site in an hour.

$9,500. *Could this possibly be true?* Two weeks later, they signed the papers to their first real estate investment, one that they have watched increase in value nearly fifteen times in a few short years through development — development in the form of their home which was designed and built in 1975 at a total cost of $58,000. Extensive saving and thrift since their marriage in 1973 made the land purchase possible, but never in their wildest imaginations did they predict such a "find" in land price in such a desirable area. Had they not been curious (or naive) enough to make that telephone inquiry, they would very probably be living in a nice enough home valued in the $60,000 range, but not one conservatively valued at $150,000 on which their mortgage is less than $40,000.

PRIMARY LESSONS FOR THE REAL ESTATE INVESTOR

The primary lesson that should be learned from their experience is that *excellent values in real estate can be found, oftentimes where you least expect them.* It goes without saying that this applies to the would-be investor as much as it does to the would-be home builder because both are investments in the real sense of the term. You should *never,*

ever be afraid to inquire as to the asking price and *never*, *ever* hesitate, any longer than absolutely necessary, to make that inquiry.

The Haddon good fortune resulted, at least partially, from *a forced sale.* Everything clicked in their favor — timing, price, opportunity, need and yes, some beginner's luck. Had they simply bought the land for investment purposes alone, it would have returned at least 25% per year, based upon current land prices in their location.

One of the most important rules for the beginning real estate investor is this: *invest only in your own backyard.* This simply means stay away from lucrative-sounding investment deals in some far away *paradise-in-the-making*, unless you plan to use the land for a second home. Stick with land in your area, especially if you intend to invest in single or multiple family dwellings for rental purposes. The best rule of thumb is to *invest only in an area about which you are knowledgeable.* If you've lived in a community for several years, you should know the good areas, potential sleepers, and past growth patterns. You would also know most of the zoning restrictions and trends and have a feel for your city administrator's actions on zoning issues. You can't stay abreast of such matters if your real estate holdings are located 2,000 miles away in Utopia.

It has been said that the right time to invest in real estate is the present time. Based on the increasing demand for apartments and other multiple-family dwellings as well as the growing need for industrial and commercial properties, the right time should exist well into the future. If you proceed cautiously and informatively, you should make a better-than-average profit.

INVESTING IN UNDEVELOPED LAND

Many land speculators buy cheap land in undeveloped areas where future development seems probable "out where the population ain't." There is, of course, solid merit to this approach, but it has drawbacks. If the future occurs too far away, prospects for profit could be negated by tax and interest payments on the property and, in some instances, liability insurance premiums. If the probability never pans out, it could result in a total loss which small investors can't handle.

The best approach is to buy good land in an area where development has already started. Such a conservative strategy will reduce your chance of loss tremendously and still give ample potential for profit, especially as the land in the developing area becomes harder to come by.

Most advisors agree that the following rules help reduce risks in real estate investments. You will have no difficulty recognizing their application to the purchase of developed land (apartment buildings, homes, commercial and industrial property).

1. Buy in your own backyard for reasons already discussed. *Don't* invest in some far away Utopia unless you intend to use the land yourself.
2. Don't buy on a purely speculative basis. Your annual investment checkup should show a *profit*, at least on paper.
3. Time your investment carefully. If you know an area is going to be developed and you have a *feel* for the politics involved, you should have sufficient time to jump on the investment bandwagon. Land prices generally require several years to mature.
4. Watch for forced sales. If a seller is anxious to sell, he may be willing to strike a bargain. Never, ever be afraid to inquire or dicker, and don't hesitate to make your move when the opportunity presents itself. Many owners eager to sell occasionally accept 20% less than their asking price. Try it, you may be pleasantly surprised.
5. Always ask yourself, "What might make the land price go up?" If you know the area as well as you should and you're tuned in to the local political and business climate, your appraisal will be accurate.

6. Use "leverage" — *the use of borrowed money*. The less money you are required to put down on any deal, the greater your leverage — and the greater your potential return will be. An example best illustrates this point.

   Jim Smith bought a parcel of land in 1976 for $4,000 with a $200 down payment. Four years later, Jim sold his land for $10,000 — a profit after expenses of over $5,000, or 25 times his *original* investment. Sellers are often willing to finance the balance after a minimal down payment in order to prorate the capital gains (the seller's profit) taxes over the term of the mortgage.
7. Is the deal likely to double in value in 5 years? Many land investors require a probable doubling in 4 years. Unless taxes are extremely low, you should be able to project a 20% increase in your investment per year. Such a projection would not apply to developed real estate generating income (rental properties).
8. Avoid subdivided tracts for investment purposes. They make great home sites, *period*. The developer of such tracts has already beat you to the punch from an investment standpoint. You would only be adding to his total profits.
9. Develop a "feel" for directions of growth in your area. Trends don't change overnight. Read the sections of your daily newspaper that generally deal with such issues. You can't invest wisely if you aren't well informed.
10. Team up with a good real estate broker in your community. You don't have to go into business with him, just get to know him. Discuss your plans candidly. His services are well worth the nominal fees usually charged.

INVESTING IN DEVELOPED REAL ESTATE

Investing in rental properties is becoming increasingly popular for the small investor. The return on investment can be great for those who don't mind being a part-time landlord, and even greater for those who are adept and willing enough to handle many fix-up jobs themselves.

Rental property, at least for investment purposes, should not include single-family dwellings. Prospective income from rents for even the better-than-average appreciating unit would not normally meet your mortgage payments, much less bring in a profit. Apartments, duplexes, other multiunit buildings, commercial and industrial properties are where profits can be made by the small investor and sometimes they can be considerable. Keep in mind, however, that an investment in rental property is going to require an investment of your time. Unless you're willing to make the sacrifice — or hire a firm to manage it for you — you'd better think twice about rental property as an investment medium.

There are three prospective sources of income in rental property: (1) the obvious, *rental income,* (2) *long-term capital gains* — profits due to the forces of inflation and appreciation, and (3) *considerable tax advantages.*

Perhaps ironically, **rental income** is not the predominant source. If rents are sufficient enough to meet expenses, you probably have a bargain. Remember that the costs of maintaining rental properties have risen tremendously in recent years, and they're likely to continue well into the future.

Long-term capital gains — profits in the future — make rental properties lucrative investments. As a rule, multiunit rental properties do not increase in value as much as a single-family dwelling and usually increase only about 2-4% per year, depending on location, condition, etc. However, continued inflation and appreciation through improvements you make yourself can increase the value more.

Tax advantages are many, and in some situations can turn an otherwise losing investment in rental property into a paper gain, especially for those in higher tax brackets. Anyone, regardless of tax status, enjoys the benefit of deducting an allowance for depreciation. The most common method of taking the deduction is called *straight line depreciation* where the total value of the rental property (not including the land on which it sits) is divided by the number of years allowed for depreciation and the resulting amount is deducted each year. Deductions for appliances and equipment used in such buildings may also be depreciated. And if all deductions exceed income from rents, the loss may be applied to your other income. Tax advantages also manifest themselves when you sell rental property, assuming the sale occurs more than 12 months after purchase: 60 percent of the difference between depreciated cost and selling price of rental property is exempt from taxes. The *obvious* tax deductions — interest payments on the loan — add to the tax benefit bundle available to the investor in rental properties.

One of the biggest reasons that more and more people are seeking financial security in developed real estate investments is the degree of control they are able to exercise in making their potential profits grow. Aside from selecting the best track-proven stock possible, investors in the stock market have no control over the multitudinous forces that dictate winning and losing on the *Big Board* (New York Stock Exchange) — and results over the past few years haven't been encouraging, especially for the small investor.

A little common sense will go a long way in dictating a "win" in rental property investments, and reducing the chance of loss considerably, For example, you would not buy a home for yourself in an area where property values are steadily decreasing. The same applies to rental properties, although stable property values in a good location is about equal. Good old common sense would also dictate that you start small, preferably with a two- or three-unit building. You should also buy in an area where there are no rent controls and where you are tuned in to community issues that could affect your investment. You certainly would not want to buy a home in an area about which you know little or nothing.

Starting small is of utmost importance. You may not earn much in terms of rental income, but you'll reap a goldmine in terms of knowledge. The best start for the small investor would be with a two- or three-unit duplex or triplex in an established neighborhood where stable or rising real estate values (*and no rent controls*) predominate. Don't invest in a new building — construction costs today have forced prices too high. A well-chosen 20-year old triplex will provide rental income sufficient to meet costs while assuring future profits from its sale — and immediate tax advantages.

As a rule of thumb, rental property should cost no more than 100 times its total monthly rental income (rent from all rental units combined). For example, a duplex selling for $60,000 should produce at least $600 per month in rents. Rental units in good locations can be found costing less than 100 times their monthly rental income which simply creates a better cash flow (money from rents to meet expenses). Monthly rental income from otherwise good rental property equal to less than 1/100th the asking price does not necessarily mean avoid the purchase, provided the property has positive appreciation potential. You may be able to increase rents (to make a better cash flow situation) after purchase by making improvements. A coat of paint and wallpaper can go a long way toward justifying rent increases for existing tenants unless, of course, they have a lease preventing increases for the lease term. It is entirely possible for you to find good rental property showing a positive cash flow from the start, so the best advice is to seek out such investments until you know what you're doing. And it would be easier to sell the property if, after taking over the reins, you find that being a landlord is not your cup of tea.

Utility costs, if at all possible, should be passed along to the tenants. Rising fuel costs and electric rates are taking larger and larger chunks out of income — try not to let it be from *your* income. Unless the building is heated and cooled by a central facility with no individual thermostats, this should pose no problem. Most tenants today expect to pay these costs unless you indicate otherwise (assuming the building is not a century old with lifelong residents of similar vintage). Individual electric meters can sometimes be installed in newer buildings converted to apartments, but this usually requires considerable — *and costly* — rewiring in older units.

Prospective tenants should be screened and a lease required, usually for one year. Ask for credit and social references, even if you don't check. And a deposit equal to at least one month's rent is common. Remember that managing rental property is a business so you should *follow businesslike procedures* — maintaining good and accurate records, handling grievance and maintenance problems promptly and fairly, and so on.

If you don't like the day-to-day responsibilities of managing rental property and are willing to forego anywhere from 6 to 10 percent of monthly rents, hire a *real estate managing firm* to take care of it for you. Such firms will find tenants, collect rents, and take care of accounting matters; if you're more concerned with long-term capital gains and tax advantages than immediate rent profits, then by all means secure their services. If your cash flow is not sufficient to pay a manager the required managing fee, it may be wise to reconsider using such services, at least until you're satisfied that the bottom line on your investment is going to return the desired gains several years down the road.

Along with gaining the assistance of a reputable real estate broker in your quest for a good investment, you should also line up the services of a lawyer competent in real estate matters and values. You will not have to pay him a retainer (unless you retain him permanently), and the nominal fee usually charged for checking out, negotiating, and closing a real estate deal will save you many problems that could arise.

It is often wise to have rental property appraised by an independent appraiser if, after deciding it meets all other criteria of a good investment, you aren't convinced that the price is right. A $50 appraiser's fee could mean the difference between success and failure for the first-time real estate investor who has yet to gain financial footing in such matters. Many advisors recommend having your first property appraised, regardless of the cash flow situation or rent-to-cost ratio. The more unbiased input you can get (but not from friends or relatives), the better your chances of coming to the right decision.

One of the biggest mistakes of first-time investors in rental property is *making too large a down payment*. If you have $10,000 to invest, you should not seek an initial investment requiring more than 80% of that amount as a down payment, or $8,000. Another way of looking at it: you should have money available for the investment equal to 1¼ times the required down payment. This buffer allows for costs of appraisal, legal counsel, and contingencies which always occur incident to the purchase of real estate.

Remember, too, that the lower the down payment, the greater the *leverage* — and the greater the return on initial investment when you "cash in" in future years. A down payment of $10,000 on a $100,000 rental property gives 90% leverage — your *weight* of $10,000 is *lifting* the entire $100,000 amount to your benefit. Assuming the cash flow meets expenses and discounting the effects of tax advantages for the moment, a 10% increase in value of the property over the next four years would double your initial investment (an average yield of 25% per year on your initial $10,000 down payment). Even if you had the property managed by a professional firm during this period, the tax advantages would more than likely keep your return on investment around the 25% per year mark, and 60% of your profits after sale (after deducting depreciated costs) are tax exempt.

Big profits are made by using the leverage principle and reinvesting profits in larger and larger rental units. Gaining the longest possible mortgage terms at the lowest interest rate you can find goes hand-in-hand in making leverage pay off to its fullest. Long-term loans requiring the smallest monthly payments will strengthen your cash flow situation, and many sellers interested in avoiding capital gains taxes all at once will finance the property personally at a rate of interest less than you could get at a loan institution. Many sellers will also carry a second mortgage on property if first mortgage money is insufficient to make the deal. You should keep in mind that with larger rental properties everything increases — potential losses as well as potential gains, including the time involved in managing the property, *so be wary.*

Investing in real estate of any kind, developed as well as undeveloped, can be a rewarding experience. If you go about it carefully, cautiously, and informatively, it will provide you with a sense of security known only to those who are privy to the commitment. No ingredient is more important than common sense in making your real estate investments grow — and reducing risks.

Will Rogers is generally credited with saying about land, "They ain't making any more of the stuff." From an investment standpoint, there is probably no better way to make your investment dollars grow . . . and just possibly wind up with a small fortune.

CHAPTER SEVEN

REAL ESTATE INVESTMENT TRUSTS (REITs)

REAL ESTATE OWNERSHIP WITHOUT HASSLE

For those investors who desire the growth potential available in real estate but not the idea of becoming a landlord, *real estate investment trusts* may be the investment medium right for you. Called REITs (pronounced "reets") and at one time a very lucrative investment medium, these trusts invest in mortgages and income-producing properties or a combination of the two.

The yield from REIT investing *can be* considerable since by law they must distribute most of the earnings. Shares in REITs are traded in the stock market at whatever price investors are willing to pay in much the same way other stocks are traded. As a closed-end investment company, REITs issue only a limited number of shares, but their availability is at par with that of any such fixed capitalization medium.

Gains on investments are paid to shareholders in the form of dividends. Management and track record are extremely important considerations when considering REITs as an investment medium. Equally important for the first-time investor is understanding how different REITs invest capital for the benefit of shareholders.

REITs can be divided into two major categories, characterized according to how capital (your dollar) is invested:

      1. Mortgage REITs; and
      2. Equity REITs.

Mortgage REITs: These are primarily short- or long-term mortgage lenders, providers of loans for developing apartments, condominiums, office buildings and similar income-producing properties. In their heyday of the early 70's, Mortgage REITs prospered. But inflation levels of the mid to late 70's forced most of the original "fixed-rate" mortgage lenders out of business. Those that escaped bankruptcy converted to an Equity (ownership) arrangement, and nearly all Mortgage REITs today participate — or at least retain the right to do so — in successful properties.

Equity REITs: Equity REITs are primarily owners (landlords) of income-producing properties. Capitalization is based on shareholder investment — there is (usually) no attempt to secure greater capitalization by acting as a financial intermediary. Investing in several good, track-proven Equity REITs can provide the safety and diversification necessary to meet your financial goals. Diversification comes from pooled ownership of many income-producing properties in much the same way mutual funds provide diversification with respect to stocks.

Choosing a REIT: The 5 general guidelines that follow will help reduce the risks of selecting investments in REITs. Keep in mind that REITs provide income in the form of dividends. While growth potential certainly exists, most advisors consider REITs as *an investment medium for current income.*

      1. Stick with *Equity* REITs, or at least REITs in which a minimum of 80% of its capital is invested in direct income-producing properties.

2. Invest in REITs backed up by large, well-known companies. Although this is no guarantee that management will be sound or that success will follow, the larger corporations are able to invest your money in real estate with money borrowed at the most competitive interest rates.
3. The REIT should have a proven track record. If yields have been keeping up with or beating inflation, the chances of continued success are evident.
4. The REIT should show a favorable *price-to-earnings ratio*. Comparison should be made to other, similarly invested REITs and, to the greatest extent possible, to stocks invested in similar industries. Read the section under *Stocks* describing how to compute the *P/E* ratio.
5. Select a good broker to advise and assist you. If the REIT you're interested in is listed on the New York or American Stock Exchange (the bigger ones are), any of the larger brokerage houses can offer assistance. Don't just walk in the front door of such firms and ask for help. Call ahead and ask for an appointment with the brokerage manager. Explain your goals and resources openly. Remember, *you want a broker interested in helping you* invest wisely in REITs, not one interested only in Blue Chips and bankrolls of corporate investors. A branch manager interested in your future business will steer you to someone best qualified and able to help.

   The choice of a competent, interested-in-you broker/advisor can't be stressed enough, whether you are investing in REITs or common stocks. There are brokers who'd rather not give the small investor the time of day. His salary is based on generated commissions, and unless you plan to invest heavily at first, he won't be able to plan an early retirement on commissions from your premier investments. Don't go with a broker until you're satisfied that he is right for you. You should feel completely comfortable with him and he should be handling several similar accounts with *proof of success.*

If you think REITs are right for you, get as much background information as possible, even before contacting a broker. There are several good books on the subject and many brokerage houses provide free publications covering the basics of REIT investing. Prospectuses and annual reports, available from the trust itself or from brokerage houses handling them, provide an inside look at objectives. Ratings and investment quality of many REITs are covered by such financial services as Moody's and Standard and Poor's. *Realty Stock Review*, a bimonthly newsletter, is considered by many to be the last word on Real Estate Investment Trusts, but its subscription price — almost $200 a year — is prohibitive for all but the serious, committed investor.

CHAPTER EIGHT

STOCKS

INTRODUCTION

For those who have the temperament and patience to withstand the ups and downs of the stock market, investing in common stocks may well be the best hedge against inflation around. The obvious assumption is, of course, that investment is made in well-chosen companies.

The stock market can not compete with real estate in growth of investment potential, but it does offer a sound, proven method for increasing the basic value of your dollar, and pay dividends as well. Investing in stocks, unlike real estate, requires no overt management on your part once the investment is made. In fact, you have no effective control over how your invested dollar will be used, a primary reason why many families are turning to income-producing real estate where their ability to control the outcome is more direct and visible.

One of the most important points for the would-be stock market investor to keep in mind is that *there are no absolute rules for success in this medium*. The very fact that there are so many stock advisory services, each basing their advice on a multitude of technical and variable information and each trying to out-perform the other, bears this out. One of the largest and most widely used of these advisory services bases its stock market forecasts on what is termed *random walk selection* — that is, results through diversified investing in randomly selected stocks will equal results of even the most analytically selected stocks. You may be surprised to learn that random walk theorists have frequently outperformed the *DJI* and other, more technical advisory services.

There are two good ways for the small investor to become a stockholder: (1) consistent, regular purchasing of shares of common stock through a stockbroker, and (2) consistent, regular purchasing of shares in mutual funds (mutual funds will be discussed later). Shares may sometimes be purchased through banks and other similar institutions, and oftentimes through places of employment. Purchases made through means other than a stockbroker generally provide a limited selection, but you can save on sales commissions. You can also save on commissions by going through a *discount broker*, but you'd better know which stocks you want because their advisory services are minimal.

There are two kinds of stock — *preferred* and *common*. Both provide a means of investment growth over the long-term, and both share in company equity. However, preferred stockholders receive fixed dividend amounts and would be one step ahead of common stockholders in rights to a company's assets in the event the enterprise turns sour. Unless you plan to invest in companies demonstrating no track record upon which to base investment decisions, you should stick to common stocks in companies with a good track record, reasonable dividend history, quality management, and one in which economic indicators suggest it will continue to do well. More on this point later.

You should also be aware that there are basically two types of stock, or more specifically two types of companies that capitalize (acquire funds) through stock offerings — *growth* and *cyclical*. A *growth* company is one which is typified by long, sustained periods of growth, generally through diversification of interests and reinvestment of earnings in furtherance of those interests. Investors are usually willing to buy stock in growth companies showing a higher *price-to-earnings ratio* (price of one share of stock divided by company's earnings per share for a 12-month period) simply because earnings are reinvested for long-term growth. A *cyclical* company is one whose earnings traditionally reflect an up-down, up-down pattern because of the cyclical nature of the company's interests and, in some cases, seasonal demand for its products or services. Many cyclicals are literally handcuffed to the economy, but more than a few investors trade in and out of these stocks, buying during what is believed to be low cycle, selling during highs — a risky approach indeed for those who don't know what they're doing. If your desire is long-term growth and you wish to avoid paying taxes on higher dividends, stay with growth stocks where the base value of your shares will return their high yields in later years. A general rule followed by many stock investors: *the higher the dividend yield, the lower the growth potential of the stock.* Although far from absolute, the rule is noteworthy.

It bears repeating — *there are no absolute rules for success in the stock market.* There are, however, some basic rules which will, if followed, reduce mistakes that could otherwise lead to absolute failure.

Investing in the stock market has been likened to major league baseball. Regardless of how good a team is, no one team wins all the time. The overall record determines the regular season champion, and oftentimes the first-place finisher shows more than a few losses during the year. So it is with stocks. No corporate enterprise in today's complex world is immune to losses and losing streaks — they are a predictable part of the game in any season. Whether your investment season is five years, ten years, or longer, the overall record is what counts. The rules and guides presented later will help you select stocks intelligently, and hopefully will make your investment season a pennant-winning one.

READING AND UNDERSTANDING
THE FINANCIAL PAGE

You should become familiar with the language of investing, especially with respect to reading and understanding stock price quotes. Current composite stock quotations are given in the financial section of your daily newspaper. They are not difficult to understand and provide a plethora of information in abbreviated form. The following example illustrates how the quotes are given and how they should be read:

HIGH	LOW	STOCK	DIVIDEND	YLD.%	P/E	SALES 100'S	HIGH	LOW	CLOSE	NET CHANGE
36-5/8	22-1/4	XYZ	2.10	6.6	11	6508	32-5/8	31-7/8	32	+ 1/4

The first two entries designate the high and low selling price of the stock for the year-to-date (an eighth of a point equals 12.5 cents); the XYZ Company has an annual dividend of $2.10 which, when divided by the last closing price ($32.00) and multiplied by 100 gives percentage yield — in this case 6.6 percent; the price-to-earnings ratio is 11 (current price of the stock divided by company's earnings per share for 12-month period); 650,800 shares of XYZ stock were traded (bought and sold); high and low price for the day, $32.625 and $31.875, respectively; last selling price when the exchange closed for the day, $32.00 even; and the closing price for the current day was 25¢ higher than the closing price on the previous day. The *Wall Street Journal* contains all eleven columns, but many newspapers omit several of these columns for space reasons. *Barron's*, a much respected financial newspaper published every Monday by Dow Jones & Company, provides excellent market commentary and a complete weekly summary of stock market transactions. Serious investors would be wise to subscribe to one of these publications. They are informative and take second place to none in the domain of financial newspapers.

One achieves the best by striving for the best.

CHOOSING A STOCKBROKER

Choosing a competent, interested-in-your-welfare stockbroker is no easy task and should not be taken lightly. An incompetent, disinterested broker can ruin you. At best, such an advisor would do well just conserving your investment principal.

Remember that along with executing transactions in your behalf, your broker should be a capable market advisor (unless you use a discount broker). Not that he will always be picture perfect in his recommendations — he won't. No one this side of Heaven can be. If your broker is affiliated with one of the larger brokerage houses, his recommendations most often will be backed by the in-house research department. All he has to do is match your financial situation and goals with the firm's best recommendations.

The following guides will help you evaluate and choose a good broker:

1. Call ahead for an appointment. Discuss briefly your financial situation with the brokerage manager or supervisor and ask that he arrange an appointment with a broker (also called *account executive*) best able to handle your account. Since you will probably be relying heavily on his advice, especially in the beginning, don't settle for a new broker or "broker trainee" — ask for an experienced broker. Let the rookies break in with the corporate accounts where little or no advice is required, not with you who needs all the counsel and advice you can muster. Never walk into a brokerage house cold — you'll get the *man of the day* who may or may not be interested in handling your account wisely and with your best interests in mind.

2. Prepare an outline of your financial situation and prospective goals and take it with you to the first meeting. The outline should include a listing of your assets and liabilities — to include savings, life insurance cash values, home equity, etc. *But don't show it to the broker* . . . until after he asks about your

91

financial situation. If he doesn't ask, and some won't, he does not have your best interests in mind. Look for another broker, perhaps even another brokerage house.

3. As previously mentioned, the larger brokerage houses provide research reports and study materials to back up stock suggestions. In devising a sensible investment program to meet your needs and situation, the broker should supply these reports. And you shouldn't have to ask for them. If you do and they aren't readily available and up-to-date, something's wrong. Remember that the research departments of the larger firms are extensive. All a good broker has to do is unite your situation with the investment tools best suited to it. If he is not well-informed as to what his firm has to offer — *some won't be* — then he can not advise you wisely. Be wary.

4. It should be obvious that a small investor has no business investing in speculative stocks. If a broker suggests other than *A*, preferably *A*-plus stocks (as rated by Standard & Poor's), they're too risky and he's more a gambler than a financial advisor. Seek another broker and let the gambler play with someone else's dollars, not yours. Even *A*-plus rated stocks, which are not necessarily "Blue Chips", afford no guarantees for conservation of principal and growth of equity. They do offer the safest route in the realm of stock market investing, however. And you should stick to them exclusively.

5. The broker-investor relationship is a professional one. It should be kept that way. In many ways the relationship is more poignant then even the physician-patient or attorney-client one, simply because the financial transactions between the two over the years are so great and the potential for loss so imminent. If you do not sense a true feeling of confidence and concern in your broker, it's probably not there. Look elsewhere for an advisor who will gain your confidence and who will exemplify an honest feeling of concern for your financial well-being. Don't settle for less.

Finding the right broker may be like searching for the proverbial needle in the haystack, but it will be a search well worth the effort. A good broker will work hard for you (and your money), regardless of how small your account may be. He won't move you in and out of stocks just to increase his commissions. He will never put you in speculative stocks. He'll call you on weekends if Monday would be too late. In essence, he'll watch over your investments as though they were his own because if you make good, he makes good. Don't settle on a broker until you're convinced that he's *your* man, not just the "man of the day."

SELECTING STOCKS: GUIDELINES

Most small investors with a sizable savings account and healthy savings program should be looking for long-term growth of capital in their stock selections. The phrase "long-term" may mean five years, ten years, different periods to different people, but certainly leading to a financial nestegg for future use (such as during retirement years). Many investors require a combination of long-term growth of capital as well as short-term income in the form of dividends. A good rule of thumb: *if you don't need the dividend income, don't invest for it.* Stay with growth stocks where the "dividends" will become manifest when you need them, not before. A good financial advisor — your broker in most cases — will be able to help you establish what might be preliminary goals at first, especially with respect to your need for present income over future capital growth.

Investing for the long-term does not mean buying shares in a few companies and sitting on them forever and ever. It's going to take work on your part as well as your broker's to produce the yield that you want. You certainly wouldn't expect the yield of a planted garden left unattended during the growing season to equal that of one carefull., worked to fruition.

Remember that no one enjoys guarantees of success in the stock market. There are certain guidelines, however, that will make your investment objectives more attainable and your labor toward that end one of love and conviction. If you follow these guidelines carefully, then maybe, just maybe, you won't lose your shirt.

1. Choose stocks rated *A*-plus by Standard & Poor's. *This is the cardinal rule for the small investor*, whether you're investing $1,000 or $10,000, in lump sum or in a monthly investment program. Investing in any lesser rated stock approaches the realm of speculation, a realm for only those who can afford to suffer complete loss of investment capital. There may be circumstances where *A* rated stocks, destined for *A*-plus rating, should be considered, but only if your broker can substantiate such destiny with extensive market research. You should keep in mind that the main elements of Standard & Poor's ratings are the histories of the various company's earnings and dividends. The *A*-plus rated companies provide a sufficient selection of investment mediums to give you diversified investments, so why settle for less. Don't settle for less, at least until you're sure of what you're doing.

2. Diversify your stock purchases. If you have $200 per month to invest, spread it out in several well-selected, *A*-plus companies. Such an approach for the small investor may mean buying fractions of shares, but it is possible through many brokerage houses. You won't actually get the stock certificates under such purchase agreements — the brokerage firm will keep them in trust for you (don't worry, they're insured). If your stock selections are diversified between several growth companies, *dollar-cost averaging* may be a perfect method of allocating your invested dollars. This simply means that you would buy more shares (or fractions of shares) when prices are low and fewer when prices are high, thereby reducing the average price of all shares purchased. It may be wise, depending upon market

conditions, to vary your invested dollar allocations — some months buy more XYZ, less WXY stock. The following guidelines will explain this approach more fully.

3. Trade only in the direction of the long-term market trend. Well-chosen common stocks will more than likely follow the market trend over the long term. If the market is rising (a bull market), most stocks — the kind you're interested in — will follow suit. The same follow-me pattern will normally prevail in bear markets (a falling market). Be wary of any broker who advises buying stocks in extreme, long-term bear markets because even the best, according to history, follow along. Temporary declines are common, expected — and usually the time to buy.

If there appears to be a contradiction between trading only in the market direction and the virtues of dollar-cost averaging as discussed in "2" above, there is. Dollar-cost averaging works in bull markets and presupposes *temporary* falling markets will intervene. Long-term bear markets are no place for small investors, or anyone else for that matter.

4. Cut losses short; let profits ride. If it is obvious that XYZ corporation is losing more than it is gaining and taking your invested dollars with it, get out. Sell. Don't wait, because tomorrow the bottom may drop out (as far as XYZ is concerned). A good rule of thumb followed by many successful investors is to sell a stock at such time as its price drops 15% below the purchase price. If you are diversified sufficiently, the loss will average out. The important point is to get your money into more promising issues as soon as possible. Admit the loss and go on.

If, on the other hand, you are enjoying gains from your stock investment, let it ride. Never cash in a winning ticket until you are ready for the prize, so long as the market is strong and indications are that it will continue that way.

5. Invest in companies that are inflation-resistant. The company that can keep costs of operation in check during inflationary times stands a better chance of continued growth from a net worth standpoint than the company whose costs of operation are tied to inflationary forces. The ideal company (in which to invest) is the one where labor costs are relatively low, raw materials are readily accessible, a high rate of return on invested capital is evident, and there is little outstanding debt (long-term debt) compared to similar industries. The research departments of most brokerage houses can come up with a list of companies meeting these criteria, so don't overlook it.

6. Look for companies where the products or services are *in constant demand*, even when poor business conditions prevail. Invest only in companies that are well-positioned in the economy and which have a firm foundation compared to others in similar industries. Stay away from those that are most susceptible to outside forces such as consumer pressure groups, antitrust actions, oil embargos, and the like. Your broker will be the best source of advice in these matters, at least until your knowledge of the stock market and its many nuances matures.

7. Confine your purchases to companies that appear *best able* to sustain above average earnings growth for at least five years, preferably longer. An investor in a company whose earnings begin to grow rapidly stands a good chance of gaining from the basic stock price-per-share increase and dividend increase (ideally reinvested). For example, a share of stock bought at $10 and paying $1 per share in dividends would quadruple in value if the price per share rose to $20 and paid $2 per share over the investment period. Finding such a company is not easy, but it will probably be leading its industry and will show a record of increasing sales volume over the past five-year period.

8. The price-to-earnings ratio, compared to the multiple (P/E ratio) of companies in similar industries, should be such that there appears to be plenty of room for future growth. Many investors make the mistake of buying stocks based only on the P/E ratio. They figure that if it's priced at six times earnings, it's a good buy. Not necessarily so. The P/E ratio of any stock is, at best, a relative yardstick, one of many indicators. You need to know whether a stock's P/E ratio is higher or lower than its past relationship to the stock market as a whole. If the ratio over the prior five-year period is, for example, 12% lower than the Dow Jones Industrial average, and it is currently 15% below the DJI, the stock is probably (again, probably) undervalued and could be a good buy. Always remember that the P/E ratio is but one bit of evidence for consideration, not the whole verdict. There must appear to be plenty of *prospects for future growth*, prospects that are likely to encourage rather than discourage other investors to invest and force up the net value of your stock's worth.

LEARN THE ROPES BEFORE YOU INVEST

There are many stock market practices with which you will become familiar that have not been discussed because they are not intended for the small investor. For example, *puts* and *calls* are options which may be purchased on stocks giving the investor the right to buy or sell a certain stock at a specified price within a specified time period, usually 30, 60, or 90 days. A "call" is bought when the investor believes the stock price will rise; a "put" is bought when it is believed the price will fall. Since the option gives the investor the right to buy or sell at or near the stock's price when the option was purchased, he stands a chance to gain considerably, provided the stock does what was anticipated during the option period. If the option is not exercised (meaning the stock did not do what was anticipated when the option was purchased), it's lost.

Under some circumstances, an investor may actually use his broker's credit to buy a stock, provided a *margin account* has been established with the broker beforehand. Margin-buying does provide a means of leverage — using borrowed money — but it is not for the beginner in the world of stock investing. The Federal Reserve System establishes the limits of margin accounts in this country.

These practices and others may someday fit into your scheme of operation, but definitely not until you and your broker have become a successful team. The basics of investing in stocks must first be learned before you embark upon the tricks of the trade, and there are many.

Surprising to most are the free opportunities available to learn the rudiments of investing. Some brokerage houses give mini-courses in investing from time to time, usually at no cost, or they charge for workbooks only. High schools, technical schools, and colleges offer short courses, often in night sessions, at minimal cost to the student. And many civic organizations sponsor these courses occasionally. Look around, inquire, use your telephone directory — you're bound to turn up at least one such opportunity in your area. If not, suggest the idea to a local brokerage house. It may surprise you when they decide to offer such a mini-course on your recommendation (but it will surprise them more for not thinking of the idea sooner because it's bound to increase their business).

Investing in stocks is risky business because so much can go wrong in today's complex world. If you will follow the guidelines as discussed in this chapter, you will probably do better than average. The problem with which you will have to cope, however, is that the average may not keep pace with inflation. But then neither can anything else.

If you would like to receive general information on investing in the stock market, write to the New York Stock Exchange, Investor Service Bureau, 11 Wall Street, New York, NY 10005.

CHAPTER NINE

MUTUAL FUNDS

INTRODUCTION

A mutual fund is an open-end investment company (one that does not have a fixed amount of capital stock) formed by a large number of persons who pool their resources for stock market investing. There is probably no better investment medium for the small investor to assure that his dollars are well diversified, and professionally managed. When you buy into a mutual fund, you are buying a cross-section of all the stocks and bonds that the fund is invested in.

One of the biggest mistakes mutual fund investors make is believing that the medium is fail-safe because of the diversity and management. The stock market decline of 1973-74 taught us a lesson — or should have — about stock market investments generally and mutual fund investments specifically. Mutual funds, on the whole, dropped more than the stock market during this period, and only about 10% of all such issues traded on the New York Stock Exchange showed a gain for investors.

The lesson, and you should entrust it to memory, is that *investing in mutual funds does relieve the investor of the chore of selecting individual securities, but not of the risks of owning them.* Fund management, for the most part, was not the primary reason for the 1973-74 decline in fund values. The market as a whole was the primary culprit because virtually all securities nosedived. Funds committed to one particular type of securities (such as growth stocks) suffered most; funds able to switch to more "liquid" investments fared but little better.

An understanding of the types of mutual funds and the investment objectives of each will help you decide which, if any, deserves your investment consideration. But first, you should learn the difference between *load* and *no-load* mutual funds.

LOAD vs. NO-LOAD MUTUAL FUNDS

Mutual funds may be purchased (1) through sales representatives who earn a commission on each sale, called a *load fee*, and (2) directly from the mutual fund investment company where no commission is charged. There is an obvious advantage to investing in no-load funds: 100% of your invested dollar goes to work for you immediately, whereas in most load funds only about 91% of your *invested* dollar is actually invested.

The actual percentage commission rate can be computed by looking at the price quotes for mutual funds found in the financial sections of daily newspapers or in financial publications such as the *Wall Street Journal* and *Barron's*. The name of the mutual fund appearing in the quote is followed by the NAV price (net asset value per share), the offer price (what it costs you to buy a share), and finally the net gain or loss from the previous closing price. The difference between the offer and NAV price divided by the NAV price and multiplied by 100 gives the percent maximum sales charge or load fee. Subtracted from 100, this equals the percent of your investment that actually goes toward share purchases. The following example is illustrative:

	NAV	OFFER PRICE	NAV CHANGE
ABC FUND	11.11	12.14	+ .12

Difference between offer and NAV price: 12.14 - 11.11 = 1.03
Divided by NAV price × 100: (1.03 ÷ 11.11) × 100 = 9.3
Maximum sales charge, percent: 9.3%
Subtracted from 100: 90.7%

An initial investment of $1,000 in the ABC Fund would result in $907.00 going for share purchases, $93.00 for sales charges.

If the ABC Fund was a no-load fund, the entry under the offer column would be "N.L.," meaning no-load, and the purchase price would be the NAV price. Your $1,000 would buy $1,000 worth of shares, or stated in terms of shares purchased, 90 shares as opposed to about 82½ shares if the fund was of the load variety.

The obvious question is, "Why buy load fund shares at all?" There is no reason to, unless you feel an obligation to subsidize the sales representative industry. The money which would have gone to pay sales expenses had you bought into a load fund will grow right along with your no-load investment because it is a part of it. During a long-term investment period, and all things considered equal, that sales fee difference could be substantial.

No-load funds are not any less innately successful than load funds, which could be the only other reason one would choose load over no-load. Granted, there are many more load funds around, but only because the no-load funds got a late start. The coming of age of mass media advertising over the past twenty years was the divining rod of the no-load market, and their growth rate since has been rapid.

One of the main advantages of no-load funds is the ease with which the investor can move to new funds or out of the market entirely, as circumstances dictate. Some no-load funds charge a share redemption fee, usually 1% or less, but that's a long way from 8 or 9 percent that comprise the load fund sales fees.

If mutual fund investments appear to fit into your financial future, your best bet would be with a no-load mutual fund. The advantages are too great to consider anything less.

MUTUAL FUND INVESTMENT OBJECTIVES

There are enough different kinds of mutual funds available to accommodate about any investment objective one might have. Since only you know what your investment objectives are — and they may change from time to time — you should choose a fund that fits those objectives as closely as possible. If, for example, you are interested in long-term growth of capital, you wouldn't invest in a fund emphasizing income, and vice versa. If you are an overly cautious investor, you might want to stick with a fund that invests about equally in stocks and bonds to minimize risk.

Evaluate your objectives first, then match them with a fund best suited to your needs. The following is a summary of the major types of funds, named appropriately for their investment strategy.

1. **Growth funds:** Most mutual fund investors invest for long-term growth of capital, so it isn't surprising to learn that most stock portfolios of the funds are oriented toward growth companies (remember the rule of thumb from the stocks discussion — don't invest for income if you don't need it). Capital gains and dividends are normally reinvested, though you may have to request reinvestment in some cases.

2. **Maximum capital gain funds:** These funds are considered too speculative for most small investors who are primarily interested in conserving capital. They can produce fast profits, but are extremely vulnerable to losses if the stocks turn sour. When considering whether a particular fund meets your investment objectives, judge the fund's issues as though

102

you were buying the individual stocks through a broker. If you wouldn't buy them individually, you certainly wouldn't collectively.

3. **Income funds:** The emphasis in such funds is dividend income. If you need it, fine. If not, stay with a balanced or growth fund. Common stocks, bonds, and high-yielding preferred stocks are often the tools of the income fund managers.

4. **Balanced funds:** Securities in these funds are essentially the same as those in the income funds, but they are generally selected in such a manner and proportion to minimize risk. Balanced and Income funds can suffer considerably if bond prices fall over a long period.

5. In addition to the four funds discussed above, there are **Specialized funds** that confine their investment strategy in one or two industries, and some that specialize only in short-term money market instruments — corporate bonds, treasury notes, and the like. Most such funds are excellent mediums for temporary investing, *provided short-term interest rates remain stable or rise.* They aren't considered wise investments for the long-term investor, especially if capital growth is desired.

SELECTING A MUTUAL FUND

Since the investment results of a mutual fund can show superior results one year, mediocre results the next, you should *not* base selection on just the current or past year's performance record.

The ideal fund or funds will show above average results for at least *the past five-year period*, preferably longer, to cover periods of both falling and rising stock prices. The "above average" comparison should be made to funds having similar investment objectives; i.e., growth to growth, income to income, and so on. Any of the funds which compare favorably to the group as a whole would be good investment mediums, at least from a track record standpoint. It's no guarantee that the fund's objectives will continue to be realized, but it's the best benchmark available, assuming the portfolio advisors responsible for the favorable record are still around.

When you compare performance records, be sure that you compare fund results over the same period of time. Mutual funds have not fared as well since the early 1970's as they did in their heyday of the 60's — you want to know relative results for the comparison period leading up to the present, not some period leading up to 1970. Again, use at least the previous five-year period for comparison purposes. Once you know how funds have done during both good times and bad, you'll be in a position to intelligently select the one right for you.

There are many publications and newsletters that provide detailed information on mutual funds, including names and addresses, whether they are load or no-load funds, investment objectives (also found in the individual fund's prospectuses), and most importantly, performance records. Some of these may be available in your local library or broker's office, or you can write direct to the company for information. The *No-Load Fund Investor* and *Handbook For No-Load Fund Investors* are published by No-Load Fund Investor, P.O. Box 283, Hastings-on-Hudson, NY 10706; *United Mutual Fund Selector* is published by United Business Service Company, 212 Newbury Street, Boston, MA 02116. Both companies will send you information on their publications for the asking. You can also obtain general information on mutual funds from No-Load Mutual Fund Association, Valley Forge, PA 19481 and Investment Company Institute, 1775 K St. N.W., Washington, DC 20006.

An early autumn issue of *Forbes*, a business magazine, contains the *Forbes Mutual Fund Survey* which rates funds according to past performance using an easy-to-understand $A+$, A, B, C, D and F system. Each issue of *Forbes* has an article on mutual funds as well. *Barron's* newsweekly contains quarterly reports on selected mutual funds, and your daily newspapers may carry syndicated columns on mutual fund investments. Many weekly and monthly news magazines — *Changing Times, Money, Newsweek,* and *Time* to name but a few — provide informative comments and surveys on the subject from time to time.

Your selection of a mutual fund based on past performance is not complete until you consider one additional element. Ask yourself if the investment philosophy of the selected fund, though successful in the past, is such that *suggests it will continue to do well in the prevailing and prospective economy.* Some funds react slowly in a changing economy in reallocating shareholder's investments, and some are prevented from shifting out of a given securities group at all without prior shareholder approval. For example, if you are in growth funds and stock prices fall for a period of time, you would probably be better off in funds where investment strategy provided for more liquid shifts of invested capital.

Although mutual funds are a diversified investment medium, and managers alter security holdings frequently as market conditions and the economy dictate, it is wise for the mutual fund investor to buy into two or three funds that meet his investment objectives. For example, conditions are such that lead you to select growth funds. You have selected several with good performance records in both rising and falling markets and the basic philosophy of the fund managers suggests the funds will continue to do well. A $200 per month investment would best be spent divided equally between two or three of the funds chosen. The fundamental reason for such an approach is simply to spread the risk as much as possible between funds that are doing and should continue to do well.

PARTING WITH YOUR INVESTMENT: GUIDELINES

When is the time to get out of your mutual fund investments? Two times — when you've reached your investment objective, and when the fund is no longer performing up to par. Getting out when you've reached your investment objective is easy enough to understand, but getting out because the fund isn't performing up to par requires an understanding of "par" in terms of mutual fund performance.

A mutual fund is not performing up to par when *any* of the following becomes evident:

1. When the fund loses a long-held *A* or *A*+ rating, or other high rating designation, from an unbiased, objective rating source. If you're in no-loads, the only expense in most cases will be in the form of taxes on profits. Many investors rely entirely on these ratings, moving their capital to the best-rated funds as conditions dictate;

2. When management philosophy changes. If you disagree with a change in investment philosophy — a fund usually requires shareholder approval — then switch to another that meets your own. This obviously applies if a fund decides to change investment objectives other than your own;

3. When the market on the whole is rising steadily and your fund is maintaining a slow or erratic pace. A well-managed mutual fund should be able to produce above-average results in rising markets at a fairly consistent pace;

4. When the market on the whole is falling and your fund is doing considerably worse than the average. Well-managed funds, even growth funds, should be able to alter their portfolios with sufficient speed to at least stay even;

5. When it's obvious that a long bear (falling) market is at hand. The small investor has no business in the market during such times. Get out and stay out until an upswing in the market predominates.

CHAPTER TEN

BONDS (FIXED-INCOME SECURITIES)

INTRODUCTION

When a person buys shares of stock or stock-oriented mutual funds, he is participating in the ownership of companies in which his money is invested. When a person buys a bond issued by a company or government, he is a creditor of that company or government, not a part owner as in the case of shareholders.

A bond is an interest-paying I.O.U., or promissory note. It is a means whereby corporations, governments, and various governmental agencies acquire funds without actually selling equity rights in the concern. Since a bond-holder is a creditor, his investment position is safer and less risky than that of stockholders, but his chances of gain are likewise reduced. Bonds are usually short on capital appreciation, but they do provide relative security and regular, fixed income during the period prior to bond maturity (anywhere from 90 days to 30 years or longer) or, in some cases, until bonds are paid off prior to maturity.

Bonds are quality-rated by at least two independent rating services, *Standard & Poor's* and *Moody's*. *Standard & Poor's* ratings run *AAA, AA, A, BBB, BB, B, CCC, CC, C, DDD* and D; *Moody's* ranges from *Aaa, Aa, A, Baa, Ba, B* and *C*. Any *Standard & Poor's* rating below *BBB* is considered too speculative by most banks, so you should probably stay with at least the *BBB* rated bonds since they are in abundant supply. Lower rated bonds generally pay higher interest rates — more income — but at the expense of security of principal. Should it become necessary to sell the bond prior to maturity, you may be forced to sell at a loss (of principal) if market conditions so dictate. You would, of course, lose both principal and interest if the bond issuer becomes insolvent with little or no proceeds to pay off creditors. For this very reason, many ultra conservative investors stick to federal Treasury notes exclusively because of the Treasury's resources for repaying debts, and also because default is virtually impossible. Certain tax advantages also prevail which will be discussed later.

Probably the hardest decision for the would-be bond buyer is *knowing when to buy*. The rating services remove most of the risk of buying bonds, but timing the purchase so that you pay a reasonable price, and get above average results, presents a challenge. What constitutes a reasonable price depends on a plethora of variables — income needs, tax bracket, prevailing and prospective inflation trends, availability of credit in the economy, maturity period of the issue, performance of the stock market — all of which weigh into the consideration in proportion to their affect upon your particular circumstances.

With the exception of new bond issues, bond prices almost never equal their face value. A bond is said to be *discounted* when its market price is below face value; a $5,000 bond bought for $4,500 (90% face value) would return a nice $500 in capital gains when paid off at maturity. If the bond had a coupon rate (promised interest payment rate) of 7%, the current yield would be 7.78% instead of 7% simply because the interest payment of $350 per year (7% of $5,000) is a fixed amount. The discounted price results in a higher yield for the life of the bond, and often occurs when new bond issues enter the market paying higher coupon rates. Unless discounted, the bonds would not be competitive with similar new issues paying higher coupon rates. Discounting evens things out, and keeps investors attracted.

If the same bond is selling at a *premium* for $5,500 — shown as 110 (110% of face value) in bond quotes — the current yield would be less than the 7% coupon rate. Remember that the interest payment in this example is always $350 per year; the current yield is a percentage of market price or, in this case, equal to 6.36%. The following formula may be used to compute the current yield on any bond:

$$\text{Current Yield of a Bond} = \frac{\text{Face Value of Bond} \times \text{Coupon Rate}}{\text{Market Price of Bond}}$$

Calculations for the above $5,000 bond selling for $5,500:

$$6.36\% = \frac{\$5,000 \times 7\%}{\$5,500}$$

The challenge to the bond buyer, especially of long-term issues, is in *predicting the trends of the economy in general and bond prices in particular*. If inflation prevails, interest rates generally follow along, forcing bond prices down (to attract investors) thereby devaluing the principal investment for existing bondholders. If it becomes a trend which does not reverse, the holder of long-term bonds could lose considerably if bond prices nose dive. He would still get his interest income, but it would be generated from a higher principal investment than the market trend demands.

It is all but impossible to predict exactly what will happen in the money or stock market. Too many things depend on what happens in Washington, London, Tokyo, Moscow, and other centers of the world. It is difficult indeed to even anticipate with any certainty what our own Congress or Administration is going to do, much less what other nations are going to do and how their actions will affect the investment dollar. The economics of investing is, at best, an inexact science whose trend is not encouraging to those who despair in uncertainties.

One further "bond indicator" is of primary importance and will be discussed before summarizing the various fixed-income securities that are available. Referred to as *yield-to-maturity*, it is the annual interest rate that takes into account a bond's total lifetime earnings. Simply stated, it is the interest rate, compounded semiannually, at which you would have to invest the purchase price of a bond in order to withdraw the annual interest income it is paying . . . and still have the face amount of the bond remaining at the end of the investment period (at maturity). The yield-to-maturity is primarily used to compare various bonds having varying maturity dates. New bond issues may be returning lucrative current yields compared to securities issued several years ago, but the older issues selling at a discount may be close and may actually provide more attractive yields to maturity. Unless you are a math wizard, ask your broker or bond dealer for a yield-to-maturity table covering issues in which you are interested.

SECURITIES OF THE U.S. TREASURY

By far the safest investment medium of money market, fixed-income securities are the notes, bills and bonds (all debt instruments) issued by the U. S. Treasury. They are considered so safe that they aren't even rated by the rating services (some bank bonds are similarly not rated). Generally, Treasury issues yield a percent or so less than high-rated corporate issues, but in times of severe cash needs they can be especially attractive. In recent years, interest yields on Treasury issues have risen to all-time highs, reflecting directly upon the Federal Reserve Board's attempt to strengthen the dollar on the international money market by raising interest rates.

A major "plus" for Treasury securities is their exemption from most state and local taxes (but not federal taxes). Coupled with the fact that they generally pay higher interest rates than most bank savings accounts, it makes an excellent investment medium for even the smallest investor. And since new Treasury issues can be purchased directly from the government or Federal Reserve Banks, you save on broker's commissions. Should it be necessary to purchase the issues through a brokerage house or regular bank facility handling the issues, commissions are usually quite modest — a few dollars on a $1,000 bond is common.

Treasury Bonds are issued in minimum denominations of $1,000, with maturity dates in excess of ten years. Issues are also available in $5,000 and $10,000 units. The U.S. Treasury issues bonds irregularly, so you'll have to watch the financial pages for announcements of public offerings which are usually made a week or two before they go on sale. Your banker or broker may be willing to keep tabs on such offerings for you, and the Federal Reserve Bank in your area may put you on their mailing list for notifying prospective buyers. Ask them. If you opt to buy, a five to ten percent deposit (of bond's face value) must be mailed to the issuing office, Federal Reserve Bank, or branch.

If the bond is sold on an auction basis, you can stipulate whether you are seeking purchase on a *competitive* or *noncompetitive* basis. The former means you'll buy at an amount no greater than your offer; the latter means you'll take it at the average bid price. You should also request that the bond (or note, discussed below) be registered in your name whereby interest payments will be mailed directly to you. A bond issued to "bearer" is payable to the bondholder (who won't be you if stolen) and requires that coupons be presented to a Federal Reserve Bank or branch for payment.

Treasury Notes are much like Treasury bonds in that interest is paid semiannually and minimum purchase unit is $1,000. Although offered more often than bonds, Treasury notes may be purchased in the same manner and according to the same rules as bonds. Maturity periods range from one to ten years on notes.

Treasury Bills are issued in minimum denominations of $10,000, with maturity periods of 13, 26 and 52 weeks.

Offers are usually made weekly, except on 52-week bills which are offered monthly. The relatively high minimum purchase price puts Treasury bills out of reach of most small investors, but their popularity is no less diminished because of the high return for such short periods of time.

Treasury bills do not provide for periodic interest payments to buyers. Instead, they are purchased *at a discount* on an auction basis. Noncompetitive bids are allowed but there are no guarantees on yields. If, for example, you are able to buy a $10,000 52-week bill for $9,050, your return would be 10.5%. Payment for the full face amount must accompany your order for the bill; once the sale is closed, usually a few days after the offer, the difference ($950 in this case) would be returned to you. Of course, the face amount would be payable at maturity.

All new Treasury bills are issued in book-entry form (represented by entries in the records of the issuing authority) either by a Federal Reserve Bank or branch, or by the Treasury Department. After their original issue, Treasury bills may be purchased or sold at prevailing market prices in much the same way other securities are traded.

Financial Page Quotations of Treasury bonds, notes and bills are slightly more complicated than stock quotations. The following examples will help you understand them:

| | TREASURY BONDS AND NOTES | | | | |
RATE	MAT. DATE	BID	ASKED	BID CHANGE	YIELD
7½s,	1984 Jan. n	99.2	99.6	+ .1	8.10

The coupon rate of this Treasury note (n) maturing in January of 1984 is 7½ percent, paid semiannully. A bond would have no "n" after the maturity month. The current selling (bid) price of the note is 99 and 2/32nds percent of face value ($1,000 × .990625) which equals about $990.63. The current purchase (asked) price is 99 and 6/32nds percent of face value ($1,000 × .991875) which equals $991.88. The selling price changed by 1/32nd of one percent from the day before, or 31¢, and the current yield-to-maturity is 8.10 percent. Notice that these government securities are priced down to thirty-seconds — the number after the decimal is the number of 32nds of a percent in bid, asked, and bid change columns.

	U.S. TREASURY BILLS		
MAT.	BID	ASKED	YIELD
2-1	14.57	14.43	15.55

The selling (bid) price of a $10,000 Treasury bill maturing on February 1st is discounted by 14.57 percent and its purchase (asked) price is discounted by 14.43 percent. The prices above would be $8,543 and $8,557, respectively. Return on this bill is 15.55 percent. The discount references under bid and asked headings are percentages in this case.

GOVERNMENT, GOVERNMENT AGENCY AND MISCELLANEOUS FEDERAL SECURITIES

Since revenues and appropriations are used to back up securities issued by the government other than the Treasury, a slight increase in risk is associated with such holdings. Though slight, the added risk usually results in about a percent higher yield over Treasury issues.

Short- and long-term securities are offered by such agencies and organizations as the Federal Home Loan Bank, Federal Farm Credit, and Inter-American Development Bank. A quick review of the financial pages of your newspaper will reveal most of the security-issuing agencies of the government. And these changes from time to time, depending on the monetary need.

Most issues are available in $1,000, $5,000, and $10,000 denominations. Many agencies sell their securities directly, some through intermediaries, and you may be able to avoid commissions altogether if purchased through participating banks or from the agency itself. Not all issues are exempt from state and local taxes, however, so you should inquire as to the tax status.

The plans are man's, the odds are God's. — Chinese proverb

A typical financial page quotation for the Federal Home Loan Bank securities is as follows:

FEDERAL HOME LOAN BANK

RATE	MAT.	BID	ASKED	YIELD
17.05	4-82	100.4	100.8	16.44

The coupon interest rate of this issue is 17.05 percent, maturing in April, 1982. The selling price is 100 and 4/32nds percent of face value ($1,001.25); the purchase price is 100 and 8/32nds percent of face value ($1,002.50); and the yield-to-maturity is 16.44 percent. Notice that in this example the price of the bond is higher than its face value, thereby reducing its current yield slightly.

TAX-EXEMPT BONDS (MUNICIPALS)

Bonds issued by states, counties, cities, public power districts, school districts, and similar quasi-governmental agencies are exempt from federal taxes, and in most cases from taxes of the state in which the issuing authority is located. Because of this tax-exempt status, municipal bonds generally yield several percentage points less interest than other bonds, but the *effective yield* often surpasses other issues which are subject to taxation.

The first step in deciding whether a tax-exempt bond is right for your situation is to determine how the tax-exempt yield compares with the yield of a taxable bond after taking into account the tax you would have to pay on the taxable bond's interest income.

For example, if lucrative taxable bonds are yielding 8%, you would want to know if the tax-exempt equivalent for your tax bracket would be the better buy. The tax-exempt equivalent is determined by subtracting from the taxable bond rate that portion attributable to your tax bracket. Assuming a tax bracket of 32%, the calculation would be as follows:

8% minus (.32 times 8%) = 5.44%

Therefore, investing in tax-exempts paying at least 5.44% would equal or better the rate you would get from a taxable bond yielding 8%.

If you own a municipal bond paying 5.44% and want to know what the taxable bond equivalent is, simply divide the tax-exempt rate by the difference between 100% and your tax bracket, as follows (assuming a 32% tax bracket):

5.44% divided by (100 minus 32) = 8%

Many advisors believe that anyone in tax brackets higher than 30% would probably be better off buying tax-free bonds exclusively. It is difficult, however, to foster such exclusive guidelines when the chance to buy high-yielding corporate issues at discount prices comes along.

Municipal bonds are available in $1,000 and $5,000 units, and new issues are fairly frequent. Maturity periods range from one to twenty years in most cases, with interest payments to registered owner (or coupon payments to bearer) semiannually.

There are basically three types of municipal bonds, characterized by the method the bond-issuer secures funds:
1. The "General Obligation" bond is backed by the taxing power of the issuer and usually has the highest rating of the three;
2. "Revenue" bonds are backed by the revenues of the bond-issuer, such as might be collected from toll roads;
3. "Special Tax" bonds are backed by taxes levied to pay bondholders for funds to support new construction projects in the public interest. Such bonds usually become General Obligation bonds once they are backed up by the full taxing power of the bond-issuer.

Municipal bonds offer the highest degree of safety to the investor after U. S. Government securities. You may be able to find good issues offered by quasi-governmental units in your own community. The bonds of many such units won't be rated by *Moody's* or *Standard & Poor's*, however, due to a lack of outstanding debt rather than a lack of security. The rating services generally won't rate bonds if the outstanding debt of the bond-issuer isn't at least equal to a certain minimum. You'll have to rely on the relative security of similar such issues over previous time periods. Also ask your banker or broker for advice.

A tax-exempt bond quotation resembles the following:

AGENCY	COUPON	MAT.	BID	ASKED	CHANGE
State Turnpike Auth. 6¼s		'02	94	97¼	+ ½

A $1,000 bond issued by State Turnpike Authority provides semiannual coupon payments at 6¼ percent, maturing in the year 2002. The selling price is $940 and the purchase price is $972.50, giving a current yield of 6.43%. The price changed by $5.00 from the day before. These dollar figures would be increased fivefold if the bond is a $5,000 issue.

CORPORATE BONDS

Many corporate bonds offer attractively high current yields. And since nearly all such bonds are rated by the independent rating services, the risk factor is low. The combination of high rate of return and reduced risk leads many investors to the corporate bond counter, and rightly so.

Keep in mind that corporations must pay interest to bondholders before they pay dividends to stockholders. Corporate bonds rated *BBB* or above provide an excellent investment medium, with greater returns than Treasury issues and possibly greater returns than municipals in terms of capital appreciation.

Corporate bonds are usually sold in $1,000 units with a variety of maturity periods available depending on the issue. There are always quality-rated corporate issues on market selling at or below their face (par) value which means the investor stands a good chance to realize a capital gain at maturity. Many long-term investors buying discounted issues schedule maturity dates so they fall within a period after retirement when the taxes on capital gains would be paid at a lower rate.

A variant of the corporate bond is the *convertible bond.* They generally yield slightly less than corresponding bonds of the corporation, but they provide the possibility of large capital gains if the corporation's stock rises in price. Discounted convertibles would be an excellent purchase in times when a long-term bull (rising) market is inevitable and the issuing corporation is likely to benefit from it. Convertible bondholders also share with ordinary bondholders an early claim to corporate assets if the going gets rough. One important point: *be sure you are aware of the terms of convertibility.* If the underlying stock splits or pays dividends in the form of additional shares, the number of shares you get on conversion should be increased proportionately.

An illustration of corporate bond quotations is as follows:

CORPORATION BONDS

BONDS	CURR. YLD.	VOL.	HIGH	LOW	CLOSE	NET CHNGE.
ABC 10¾ 97	11	23	95	94¾	94¾	- ¼
BCD 5¾ 87	cv	37	55¼	54¼	55¼	--

The ABC corporation bonds maturing in 1997 were issued to yield 10¾ percent interest. The current yield is 11 percent, and a total of 23 - $1,000 bonds were traded the day before. The high the day before was $950, the low was $947.50; and the net change over the previous day's close of $947.50 was down $2.50.

The BCD example represents the quotation for a convertible bond yielding 5¾ percent and maturing in 1987. The current yield of a convertible is computed by dividing the coupon rate (5¾%) by the previous day's closing price percentage (55¼%) which equals 10.41 percent.

Corporate bonds are priced down to eighths (.125 of 1 percent), unlike U. S. securities which are priced down to thirty-seconds (.03125 of 1 percent). Be sure to keep this in mind when comparing different securities.

117

GUIDELINES FOR BUYING BONDS

The following guidelines are intended to provide you with a sound approach to bond buying (investing) without sacrificing conservation of principal.

1. Invest only in bonds rated *BBB* or higher by *Standard & Poor's*. Government securities and many municipals aren't rated; the former are very safe, the latter generally safe, but be sure you investigate the financial condition of the issuing agency or quasi-governmental unit before buying. How? Ask your broker or banker and, if possible, look at past performance of similar bond issues of the bond issuer.

2. If you buy corporate bonds, buy only those issues traded (sold) on the New York or American stock exchange. The issues should also be *actively traded* on the market to provide for easy liquidation if it should become necessary before maturity. Normally, if the financial pages show that 25 or more issues are traded weekly, it is generally a good sign that the bond issue is readily marketable.

3. Look for *discounted bargains*. They offer capital gains possibilities at maturity, and protection against being deprived of several years of high yields should a corporation call in their bonds prior to maturity in order to refinance their debt at lower interest rates. Many long-term issues provide for early repayment, usually after at least a stipulated period of interest-paying time. If a bond is discounted, interest rates are higher than at the bond's par value and no corporation would refinance a debt until interest rates fall.

4. The *timing* of a bond purchase involves knowing when to buy and for how long a maturity period so that your investment dollar is put to most efficient use. For example, if you buy a quality $5,000 bond for 90% face value and it pays 6½% coupon interest, the current yield (7.22%) — $325 per year — will be your interest income during the period prior to maturity. If interest rates rise continuously during the period

prior to maturity, bond prices will generally fall forcing yields up in order to keep new investors attracted. The new investors will, of course, realize the same interest income as you, but it will be generated at a lower bond price.

If your $5,000 bond is a long-term committment and the rising interest rates are likewise long-term, you would be unable to liquidate your investment position prior to maturity (to take advantage of lower bond prices, for instance) without suffering a capital loss (the difference between what you paid for the bond and what it's selling for now to generate the higher yields new investors are demanding). If the same long-term bond had been purchased during or prior to a period of stable or decreasing interest rates, you would enjoy a stable or higher current yield than the market trend demands. Investors buying into the market during this decreasing interest period would realize the same interest income (dollar-wise) as you, but it would be generated at a higher bond price.

It is generally best to invest in long-term issues (securities maturing after 5 or more years) if it appears inflation will stabilize or recede, and in short-term issues if inflation and interest rates appear to be rising. Many advisors recommend staying as "liquid" as possible during inflationary periods, and advise buying the shortest term issues possible during this period (Treasury notes or money market certificates, for instance).

5. If your tax bracket is 30% or higher, *consider buying municipal bond issues first.* This does not mean buy only tax-free bonds, but be absolutely sure you weigh the tax advantages at your income tax bracket before committing to otherwise lucrative purchases.

6. Have an understanding of the broker's fees *before you invest.* Some charge a very nominal fee — $4 or $5. Others charge more. Ask about the commission rate before placing your order. Obviously, you would avoid commission charges altogether on new bond issues.

CHAPTER ELEVEN

ALTERNATIVE INVESTMENTS

INTRODUCTION

Investing in mediums other than those already discussed in this book can be very tricky. The requirements for such alternative investment routes are often beyond the reach of the average consumer, and the "road to riches" is paved with numerous uncertainties. Yet thousands upon thousands of Americans shun the safer waters of real estate and securities every year and venture into what can only be called *choppy waters of speculation*. Such routes, more often than not, lead to disaster and complete loss of hard-earned investment dollars.

The alternative investment mediums pursued by the majority of such investors fall within one of the following five categories:
1. Precious metals — gold and silver
2. Precious stones — predominantly diamonds
3. Art objects — paintings and prints
4. Collectibles — antiques and cultural objects
5. Chance leases — leases on federal land for oil and gas rights

There are many other areas where investors put their dollars, but these are generally considered the most common. *None are recommended for readers of this book* for obvious reasons, unless (1) you are an expert or quasi-expert in the selected field, and (2) you have access to professional advice in the field from an unbiased source in your community. Even then, it's extremely chancy and involves more unpredictability than nine out of ten consumers should reasonably assume.

Unpredictability is not the only element in such speculative investing that detracts from its appeal. In recent years especially, misleading advertisements have led many people down a rosy path to disaster. For example, the magazine ads of at least one private minter of gold coins states that their coins are a great buy compared to those coins minted by the U. S. Treasury. Although the meaning of the phrase "a great buy" is unclear, the suggestion is "a better buy" and such an understanding couldn't be any further from the truth.

How can you tell fact from fiction in advertising claims? *Too often, you can't.* If such advertisements were subject to the same scrutiny that many states impose upon insurance advertisements, you'd have little to worry about. Unfortunately, from the standpoint of the consumer, they are not. Logic does not always serve as the basis for many of our consumer protection efforts.

Although such alternative investment routes take on a slightly different meaning in terms of *safety, liquidity*, and *convenience*, it's doubtful whether any such investments would meet these criteria for the average consumer. It is literally a different world and, though the novice could learn much about it from various educational sources, his chances of mastering it sufficiently to be successful are remote.

Remember, too, that investment goals are best achieved if investment strategy includes a yearly checkup with respect to a medium's *diversity, flexibility*, and *results*. Such alternative investment mediums for the average consumer lose hands down on the first two counts and too often on the third as well.

What is the bottom line? *Stay away from these and other alternative investment mediums if you don't know precisely what you're doing.* Look at the professional ads in newspapers, magazines, and direct mail circulars, read all the hoopla of "rags to riches" stories, even buy if you must. But don't buy for investment purposes. You'll lose as sure as rain.

A brief description of these alternative investment mediums is presented in the following sections of this chapter. They are intended to be informative only, and are not guidelines for investment selection.

PRECIOUS METALS: GOLD AND SILVER

GOLD: The greatest activity of the small investor is in gold coins, although the most economical way to own gold is in pure bullion (bar) form. Probably the biggest reason gold coins are preferred is the fact that they *are* money in addition to having an intrinsic gold value. Their monetary value is assured at some level, regardless of what gold does on the world market.

There are essentially three kinds of gold coins available today:
1. **Bullion coins:** Pure gold coins the value of which is based on the price of bullion. They are usually minted in large quantities and generally cost no more than 5% of their intrinsic (gold) value.
2. **Monetary coins:** These coins are not pure gold and are often commemorative in nature. Many originate in foreign nations (where you might have to go in order to realize their value when you wish to sell). Newspapers, magazines, and direct mail advertisements are frequently used to promote these coins.
3. **Numismatic coins:** Pure gold coins minted in America prior to 1933. Rarity has forced the prices on such coins to unbelievably high levels in many cases. Many numismatic coin buyers have gotten stuck with counterfeit coins — solid gold perhaps,

123

but numismatically worthless. The numismatic value of coins minted after 1933 exists in theory, but rarely in practice.

SILVER: Silver is also available in pure bullion form, but most investors prefer the more flexible coins. Surprising to many, silver coins are often cheaper to buy due to the surcharge that many ingot dealers levy. And owning ingots can be risky if the dealer goes out of business and no other dealer *recognizes* the assay mark.

Silver is also marketed in the form of commemorative bars and collectibles (i.e., silver-plated spoons). Not only must the buyer be concerned that he is getting the silver content advertised, he must also be satisfied that the usually "limited edition" premium is worth the asking price. If it pleases his aesthetic senses, it probably is. If it is intended as an investment, it probably is not.

PRECIOUS STONES: DIAMONDS

Diamonds aren't just a girl's best friend. They are also the best friend of most small investors who dabble in precious stones.

However, according to the experts, most of the diamonds bought by investors for hoarding in safe-deposit boxes as potential hedges against inflation will do little to bring financial well-being in later years. Why? Because the gems are usually sold at an inflated price to begin with, *and the typical buyer*, more often than not, *doesn't know what he's buying.*

Diamonds are sold by weight (carat), but weight is only one factor in the valuation of a diamond. The most important factors in determining the value of a diamond, regardless of its size, are purity of its color, accuracy of its cut, and absence of flaws. To the untrained eye, a counterfeit diamond, sometimes a poorly made one, will provide a radiant sparkle sufficient to disguise its authenticity. If you want sparkle, buy sparkle. But don't buy it for investment purposes.

It is generally agreed that cut and size of a diamond should be considered together. The ideal cut of a diamond is known as the *brilliant cut*, consisting of specified proportions and angles as calculated by a physicist in 1919. Most diamonds, however, are not so cut because it generally results in a smaller carat size. And most consumers want size, not intrinsic value.

The Gemological Institute of America subdivides the color of diamonds into 23 different gradations. Unless compared to a *standard*, it's virtually impossible to determine the color differences between the grades. Since purity of color is an important factor in diamond value, and price differences up to 10% aren't uncommon from one grade to the next, it is essential that the would-be buyer knows the color grade of the stone under consideration.

There are five grades of diamond clarity: *flawless, very very slightly imperfect* (VVS), *very slightly imperfect* (VS), *slightly imperfect* (SI), and *Imperfect* (I). Imperfect stones have flaws that can be seen with the naked eye. Slightly imperfect stones usually show no flaws without optical magnification.

Investors in these rare gems should obtain as much written documentation of authenticity as possible, and deal only with reputable dealers. It is no guarantee that you'll make a profit, but it may save your capital investment in later years.

ART OBJECTS

For the most part, original paintings and quality prints comprise the interest of most small investors (and some not so small) in this category of investments.

The value of an original painting is based on many factors, the least of which is frequently aesthetic beauty. Too often, the important factors don't make much sense to the small investor, so he ignores them and buys on physical appearances alone. There's nothing wrong with buying a beautiful painting simply because it's a beautiful painting, but there is more to it from an investment standpoint than meets the eye.

Supply and demand are the most important factors when considering a painting or a print for investment purposes, and professional advice is a must (*print* refers to etchings, engravings, and lithographs which are usually signed and numbered by the artist in pencil). Supply and demand are determined by at least four factors: (1) *authenticity* — is the work authentic or a copy (or fraudulent forgery); (2) *quality* — the reputation of the artist plays an important role here, although some inferior works by great artists are often in less demand; (3) *rarity* — usually the demand for works of a great artist who painted fewer works is greater than the demand for works of a similarly great artist who painted prodigiously; and (4) the *condition* of the work of art.

Like anything else, the value of paintings and prints can also be affected by such factors as popularity trends and provenance, and neither is effectively predictable or measurable. It is difficult indeed to explain to the novice why a painting purchased by someone for $10,000 brings $50,000 at auction one year later, but it happens frequently. "Who" owned the work is often more important than even the technical and artistic quality involved.

Investing in art objects requires an intimate knowledge of not only the medium itself but of the subtleties involved. Experience is the only way to learn, but it would cost you dearly getting to the baccalaureate level. If you aren't at that level already, forget it for investment purposes.

COLLECTIBLES

A critical reader of this chapter may hasten to point out that, technically speaking, antiques are not considered "collectibles" in the finer sense of the word. The author agrees. However, they have been collectively grouped under this section for the sake of simplicity in the belief that the average reader understands the difference between "collecting antiques" and collecting cultural objects such as rare books, old records, and commemorative plates and figures.

The most common bond between antique and true cultural object collecting is *the auction block*. They are predominantly auction items, although much activity occurs through ads appearing in various trade and shop publications and through collectible dealers.

The greatest detriment to collecting antiques and cultural objects for investment purposes is the unpredictability involved. It's next to impossible to predict the subtleties and nuances that play such an important part in auction item values, and unless you're an old hand on the auction circuit, you won't be able to.

There is no question, agree the experts, that the best values are found on the auction block. The value of any item when tested on the open market is fairly assured at some level, and that tested level will usually hold up at the time of resale. But if the item shows little or no appreciation between the time of purchase and time of resale, auction commissions as high as 25% will yield a net loss to the seller.

Many unknowing collectible investors start out with a net loss when they buy junk disguised or advertised as an antique. There is absolutely no chance of gain under these circumstances, unless you resort to the same tactics in resale that resulted in your *faux pas*. You should be wary of any dealer who makes glowing promises about the prospective value of any item. You're not going to get the best deal from a dealer in the first place, because his motives are the same as yours — *profits* — but on a grander scale.

The best advice to the would-be collectible investor is "caveat emptor" — *let the buyer beware*. If you don't know what you're doing, you'd better appreciate what you buy because what you buy may not appreciate.

Nothing is constant but change. — Heraclitus

CHANCE LEASES

Consumers face a barrage of newspaper, magazine, and direct mail advertisements suggesting certain wealth and fortune to those who participate in drawings for oil and gas leases on federal lands. Although it is true that a few have struck it rich in such deals, *the chances of even winning the right to acquire such a lease are slim.* In 1980 alone, more than four million people filed for about 7,000 available federal land tracts that were up for noncompetitive bidding (odds: over 500 to 1 against winning just the right to lease). Those who did win the lease drawings faced a 90% chance that the land would never be drilled on simply because all the federal lands that come up for such noncompetitive drawings for lease rights are not located within any "known" geologic oil and gas producing areas. Those that are so located are leased through competitive bidding with the highest bid taking the lease (by the oil and gas companies).

If you think noncompetitive drawing for lease rights sounds more like gambling than investing, you're right. *It is.* But it's a gamble in which Americans by the thousands participate every other month in the hopes that maybe, just maybe, luck will shine their way. For the most part, it's a waste of time and money and it can get expensive, especially for those who use a "filing service" to aid in parcel selection and filing requirements.

It is true, however, that the lottery winner stands a better chance today of attracting the interests of major oil companies simply because the oil and gas shortage forces more speculative drilling in less desirable geological regions. If you win a lease right on a tract of land that shows any potential whatsoever, an oil company may offer upwards of $50,000 for your lease rights, not a bad return on a $10 filing fee. But the real money is made on *overriding royalties* which can be as much as 5%. If oil is found, you could wind up with a small fortune.

Based on laws of probability, it has been estimated that a lease speculator would have to file at least 25 applications per month for a year in order to win just one lease right over a 12-month period. At $10 per application, that's a hefty $3,000 outlay. Many regular lease speculators use private filing services which, for a fee, evaluate the available parcels on the basis of geological and market information and recommend tracts for which application should be made. This does not increase your chances of winning the draw, but it does increase your chances of winding up with a better tract. The exact odds on winning a lease are determined solely by the number of entries for each tract. And, naturally, the better tracts will have the most entries. The names of firms and individuals specializing as filing services can be located through business or professional associations, trade publications, chambers of commerce, and sometimes in the yellow pages of telephone directories under "Federal Leasing Services." Keep in mind, however, that such services are in no way connected with the government agency involved with land management. You can file directly with the Bureau of Land Management office located in your state. Addresses are available from the Bureau of Land Management, Department of the Interior, Washington, D.C. 20240.

Regardless of whether you file yourself or through a filing service, lease rights are good for 10 years if you win. It costs $1 per acre per year to lease the land, and tract sizes range from about 40 to 10,000 acres.

Playing the oil and gas lottery game is great if your only desire is to subsidize the federal bank account. But for those who do, remember that the chances of subsidizing your own bank account are slim indeed.

SECTION FOUR

INSURANCE

Insurance is a predictable means of protecting financial security from the unpredictable and unforeseen.

CHAPTER TWELVE

THE WORLD OF INSURANCE

INTRODUCTION

In the simplest of terms, insurance can be defined as *protection against the unintended and unexpected loss of something of value.* This loss is measured in monetary terms for insurance purposes.

It has been suggested that insurance touches the lives of almost everyone in the civilized world. Although this is a great understatement, it serves to express the situation correctly. Anything of value the loss of which would create a financial burden in replacing is the subject of insurance. In a world where inflation continues to rise, where the cost of goods and services takes an ever-increasing portion from our paychecks, where salary increases never seem to offset the spiraling cost of living, it is fundamentally important that we are able to protect against the potential loss of those things we value most.

The need for insurance protection has created one of the largest, most rigidly regulated industries in the world today, the insurance industry. With few exceptions, no other industry is as carefully regulated and scrutinized. Insurance, because it does involve interstate commerce, is entirely subject to regulation and control by the federal government. However, a landmark 1944 Supreme Court case resulted in Congress passing the McCarran Act, or *Public Law 15*, which gave to each state the right and authority to regulate insurance, so long as such regulation proved adequate and effective.

That adequacy and effectiveness through state regulation and control is being challenged by the government in the form of national health insurance. Although health care is but one area of insurance concern, it is of primary importance to us all for reasons too obvious to mention. There is no question that the majority of states have conscientiously attempted to regulate insurance, but there is serious concern that such regulation has been, or can be, effective in containing health-care costs.

The states are not alone in their apparent failure to effectively regulate insurance. National health insurance legislation is a direct attack on the insurance industry itself for not taking a more active role in cost containment and benefit standardization. The insurance industry must assume a more active role in providing quality insurance products meeting realistic insurance needs at a price within the reach of everyone.

There has never been a more important time in our history for the consumer to come to grips with the question of how to spend each hard-earned insurance dollar. The purpose of this section is twofold: (1) to describe as completely as possible the most common areas of insurance coverage that "touch" our lives today, and (2) to provide the reader with sufficient information to make the right decisions for spending that portion of income designated for insurance protection. Clearly, we can not rely completely on the federal government, the state, nor the insurance industry itself, to guide us adequately and intelligently in our quest. Because insurance does not just "touch" our lives . . . *it is an integral part of it.*

KINDS OF INSURANCE

The average consumer is concerned — *or should be* — with four kinds of insurance protection:

1. Health insurance: Protection against loss of health in one form or another due to injury or sickness.
2. Life insurance: Protection against untimely death, or as a means of providing a financial resource in old age.
3. Homeowner's (or apartment dweller's) insurance: Protection against loss of the home and personal belongings, and loss of financial security through liability for injuries sustained in the home.
4. Automobile insurance: A composite form of insurance protection covering losses resulting from the use of an automobile.

Obviously, there are many other kinds of insurance coverage today. The four listed above are the most commonly used (and misused) and are therefore the subject of this consideration. It has been estimated that 98% of every insurance dollar spent in the United States by the average consumer (exclusive of corporate insurance spending) goes for the purchase of insurance protection of the kinds listed above. Due to reasons which will become clear later, a sizable percentage of this amount is spent needlessly, even futilely. "More" is not necessarily better with respect to insurance protection. Too often, "more" results in a waste of hard-earned money, money that could be working for the consumer through savings and investments.

MAIL ORDER INSURANCE: IS IT A GOOD BUY?

Mail order insurance has been around for more than two decades, but it was not until the late 1960's that the concept of mail order insurance firmly settled itself into insurance management's scheme of operation. Today, nearly every major insurance company in the United States spends at least some of its marketing dollars in mail order solicitation. Mail order includes direct mail, newspaper, magazine, and other mass circulation mediums where no agent is involved in the transaction.

There can be advantages to buying insurance through the mail. Policy rates are generally lower because there is no agent's commission involved. Life or health insurance purchased through the mail generally requires few or no health questions to answer, and almost never requires a physical examination. And because advertising laws and regulations of all the states are becoming more and more restrictive, the consumer will find in his policy exactly what he reads in the advertisement. Nearly all companies extend a 10 to 30 day *free look* period, meaning a policyholder can return the policy to the company and have his money refunded if he is not satisfied with it for any reason. In the past few years, more and more mail order insurers are using a *send no money* marketing approach, requiring no money with the application or enrollment form. Some companies charge a small first premium ($1.00 is common) to help cover administrative costs incident to issuing a policy, but they'll return it to you upon request within the free examination period if you change your mind about buying the insurance.

The main disadvantage of buying insurance through the mail involves the lack of consumer understanding about what is being sold rather than a deficiency in the product itself. *The majority of life and health insurance sold through the mail is secondary coverage, not primary coverage.* It is intended to supplement existing insurance plans (usually group insurance plans provided through places of employment) and provide a means whereby the average consumer can "fill in the gaps" of an otherwise adequate insurance program. Such supplemental insuring efforts should be entered into cautiously and informatively — in short, with a definite plan of action in mind.

One of the gravest consumer misunderstandings about mail order health insurance involves the coverage of *pre-existing conditions.* These are simply old health problems for which you may or may not have been medically treated or advised in the past, and which are not covered by many such policies for a specified period of time after the policy is issued, usually six months to two years. It is important to note that it is not necessary for an old health condition to have been treated in the past in order for a company to deny liability for it. If the condition, or symptoms of the condition, are in existence when application for coverage is made, chances are good that no coverage for the condition will be afforded until after the pre-existing health conditions "waiting period" is served. The moral of this fact should be obvious: *don't wait for sickness or injury, or symptoms of an impending malady, to apply for insurance*, either through the mail or through an agent. And before blaming the insurance industry for what might appear to be a sure-fire escape clause in mail order insurance, keep this fact in mind: pre-existing conditions "waiting periods" in mail order policies help keep premiums low. If coverage is needed for a condition which is already in existence, seek out a reputable agent and pay the substandard premium for the coverage required. You probably won't be able to cover an existing condition at all.

Mail order insurance is here to stay. And for the most part, it's better than ever and getting better. Americans spend over a billion dollars a year on mail order insurance, the bulk of which goes for health plans, followed in order by life, automobile, and homeowner's insurance. It is unfortunate that many of these premium dollars are spent unwisely, even needlessly. But mail order insurance can be a good buy — if it is made informatively, with caution, and a plan of action based on knowledge and understanding of the insurance needs at hand. This Section will provide that knowledge and understanding.

CHAPTER THIRTEEN

HEALTH INSURANCE

INTRODUCTION

Americans spend more for health insurance than for any other kind of insurance protection. And rightly so. Health is a precious commodity upon which no monetary value can be placed. The importance of good health permeates our very existence — radio and television commercials, magazine and newspaper advertisements, sporting events of every conceivable nature radiate our health consciousness — and we would be challenged indeed to name anything more precious and desirable.

The role of health insurance is an indirect one. That is, although loss of health is not in itself a monetary loss, *it results in monetary loss* — loss of income, loss of financial security in the form of savings, loss of ability to meet all the costs brought on by ill health.

Health insurance consists of two distinct types of coverage:
1. Hospitalization plans, and
2. Loss-of-income plans, also called disability plans.
These coverages will be discussed separately in this chapter.

HOSPITALIZATON PLANS

These plans provide coverage during periods of hospitalization on either a fixed-indemnity (constant dollar) or expense-incurred (actual cost) basis. Most mail order plans are of the fixed-indemnity variety. Most group insurance plans and many agent-sold hospitalization plans provide benefits on an expense-incurred basis.

Also included in the hospitalizaton plan area are those insurance plans that require a prior period of hospitalization in order for their benefits to be payable. Most *home recovery* and *nursing home* policies require that the policyholder be confined in a hospital from one to seven (or more) days in order for home recovery or nursing home benefits to be payable. State insurance departments receive many complaints from consumers who purchase these policies believing that their confinements will be covered without prior hospitalization.

CATEGORIES OF COVERAGE, HOSPITALIZATION PLANS

Buying adequate hospitalization insurance may be the single most difficult purchase a consumer ever makes. Careful planning coupled with informative purchasing is a must.

First, a complete evaluation of the coverage you now have should be made. Most employers will provide booklets describing their insurance bencfits. Attention should be paid to plan maximums, exclusions, deductibles, and other limits to coverage. Three out of four consumers have no idea what their insurance program provides — *until too late*. If you do not work for an employer who provides a health insurance program, your dilemma may be greater but evaluation of an existing program will probably be simpler. The evaluation should be made in terms of the following four categories of hospitalization insurance programs.

Category One: Minor expenses such as occasional doctor's visits, check-ups, routine physical examinations, and normal maternity coverage *should not*, under most circumstances, be insured against. Why? Because these expenses are generally planned, anticipated costs which most families can handle themselves. Notice that "normal maternity" has been placed in this category because the premium required to provide such coverage costs more in the long run than it's worth. If normal maternity expenses are insured against, you will be paying a higher premium (in some cases, much higher) for a benefit that will be used only once or twice in a lifetime. You can buy coverage that includes these benefits, but the average consumer will save money by avoiding them.

Category Two: Insurance coverage for basic hospital and surgical costs should be provided. Benefits should be payable on an expense-incurred basis, and should cover at least an average hospital stay and average surgical procedures during the hospital stay. Benefits should also be provided to cover doctor's bills other than those of the attending surgeon. *Category Two* coverage is considered the minimum insurance protection for the average family.

Category Three: Major medical insurance coverage is generally classified as an extension of the basic provisions of *Category Two* coverage. Quality group insurance policies, such as most of the Blue Cross (hospitalization plans) and Blue Shield (surgical and doctor's fees coverage) plans, will cover both *Category One* and *Two* costs, as will better individual insurance plans. "Individual" simply refers to policies which cover individuals or individual families and which are sold on a non-group basis. *Category Three* plans should not contain a maximum limit of benefit payment per covered person of less than $50,000.

Category Four: Catastrophic expenses are those that could be encountered with long-term, expensive illnesses such as cancer, diabetes, heart conditions, and the like. Some *Category Three* policies, especially those sold on a group basis, provide for catastrophic expenses within the policy per se. Others, especially those sold on an individual basis (as opposed to group plans), require the purchase of an additional rider to provide such extended and extensive coverage. Since the chances of a catastrophic illness striking are minimal, premiums for such additional riders are generally quite low.

EVALUATING YOUR HOSPITALIZATON INSURANCE PROGRAM

Ideally, no family should be without hospitalization insurance that includes benefits of *Category Two* and *Three* discussed above, and *Four* if the purchase is at all possible (*Warning*: do not try to buy this comprehensive coverage through the mail. You can't. You can buy supplemental coverage this way, but that's all). Evaluate your program with respect to the following twelve points:

1. Your coverage should pay, *on an expense-incurred basis*, reasonable hospital expenses including room and board, surgeon's fees, laboratory and X-ray charges, medically-necessary incidentals, medicines and drugs while hospital confined, and miscellaneous charges such as recovery room that necessarily occur as a result of your malady.

2. In policies containing a *coinsurance factor*, the insurance company should pay at least 80% of the reimbursable expenses, leaving no more than 20% to be paid by you. A well-chosen supplemental policy will cover these expenses that the primary insurer doesn't.

3. Benefits for each covered person should be available up to at least $50,000 or, if the maximum applies to each period of sickness, a maximum per covered person of at least $25,000.

4. If the plan provides for catastrophic expenses, a maximum per covered person equal to at least five times the basic maximum exclusive of the catastrophic provision.

5. The hospital room and board rate should be generous enough to cover the average rate charged in your geographical area, or at least near this average. A supplemental plan can make up the difference.

6. If the coverage is through group insurance, you should have the right to convert to a similar individual plan without further evidence of insurability if you leave the group. And you should be able to continue coverage in some fashion during lay-offs, upon retirement, and your family should have some continuation rights upon your death.

7. There should be no unusual exclusions to coverage. For example, the moral exclusions of years gone by such as treatment for alcoholism, drug addiction, attempted suicide, and venereal disease are generally not excluded in better policies today. However, some well-known companies still use these exclusions in their policies, so you'll have to weigh their significance in relation to your needs.

8. Coverage should be provided for *complications of pregnancy* in policies intended for protection during child-bearing years. Coverage for normal pregnancy can be expensive, as discussed earlier, and is not usually recommended.

9. Coverage for newborn infants, if the policy contemplates such coverage at all, should be provided from the moment of birth. Many states require such moment of birth coverage, and the better plans provide for it everywhere whether required or not.

10. If the plan is purchased individually (not through a group), the insurance company should not be able to cancel your coverage "at their option." The plan should be guaranteed renewable to at least age 65. A company may have to raise premiums on guaranteed renewable policies at some time, but the increase can't be applied to just one family. Such an increase must be applied to all members of a like classification residing in your state of residence.

11. Deductibles are desirable because they save money,

oftentimes substantially. You will have to determine what deductible is right for your circumstances and income. Keep in mind that although a larger deductible reduces your insurance cost, it can put families in a bind meeting expenses during the deductible period.

12. If you must purchase non-group coverage, *shop around for the best buy.* All things equal, premiums for similar coverages can vary by as much as a hundred dollars or more per year, depending on the company. Based on 1982 estimates, you can expect to pay at least $80 to $90 per month for comprehensive *Category Two* and *Three* coverage for a family of three, and this premium would probably be a bargain.

The twelve points discussed above should serve as a guide in evaluating your family's hospitalization insurance program. If your evaluation (comparison) reveals too many deficiencies in significant areas of coverage, you should consider increasing present coverage, if possible, to remove the deficiencies or consider another company's plan. If your insurance program was purchased through an agent, discuss the deficiencies with him. An independent agent represents many companies, and if there is no possible way to up-grade with the present insurance company, he can suggest another to meet your family's health insurance needs.

If you are insured under group insurance, such as that provided by employers, and your evaluaton reveals deficiencies in significant areas of coverage (moment of birth coverage for newborn infants is not a significant area of coverage for a family past the child-bearing years), it might be wise to consider supplementing your coverage with a non-group policy. The deficiencies of most group policies can be offset economically by the purchase of fixed-indemnity policy paying a flat dollar amount for each day of hospital confinement. For example, if your group policy (or comprehensive plan purchased individually through an agent) meets the guidelines above, but the hospital room and board rate is below the average rate charged in your geographical area, you can purchase a fixed-indemnity plan to cover you and your family in an amount needed to supplement present coverage. In other words, you can buy (and pay for) only what is needed to up-grade your total hospitalization insurance program without buying (and paying for) benefits you already have. This is important: *determine where the deficiencies are, what is needed to remove them, and buy only what is needed to up-grade to the desired level of protection.*

Mail order insurance is primarily supplemental insurance, and can be an excellent way to up-grade your coverage at low cost. Finding a mail order policy to meet your needs should pose little difficulty, since most insurance companies use the major newspapers frequently to advertise their products. Weekend newspapers are the most commonly used medium, especially on Sundays. A better, little known way to secure such coverage is to write or call the policyholder service department of a known mail order insurance company licensed in your state and request information and an application for the coverage you need. Most state insurance departments will supply you with a list of insurance companies licensed in your state that offer such plans, but they are generally forbidden to recommend one company over another. They will, however, tell you which companies to stay away from.

Whether you supplement your present insurance with a mail order plan or one purchased through an agent, *be sure the supplementing policy pays in addition to other insurance coverage.* Some policies will not pay benefits if another policy pays most of the costs. Don't buy a plan to supplement existing coverage that doesn't pay you (or the hospital if you assign benefits) the full daily benefit for which you are paying premiums.

LOSS-OF-INCOME PLANS

These plans provide benefits during periods of disability due to injury or sickness, without regard to a previous

145

period of hospitalization. Their primary function is to *replace an income* which is lost during the disability period, and some plans pay such benefits for life. Most companies writing loss-of-income plans will not insure you for more than 75 to 80 percent of present monthly income (e.g., if you are making $1,000 per month, you could only buy coverage providing $750 to $800 per month). A good insurance program would include, in addition to comprehensive hospitalization coverage, a well-planned loss-of-income policy to protect against lost wages due to injury or sickness.

EVALUATING YOUR LOSS-OF-INCOME INSURANCE PROGRAM

Not too many years ago, insurance advisors considered loss-of-income protection to be fundamental protection. With no hospitalization insurance, a person could still meet the expenses of a long disability if he was insured by a good loss-of-income policy paying an adequate monthly benefit. *But not today.* Costs of hospitalization have risen so much in recent years that a single day in the hospital can cost as much as an average disability policy pays in a month, especially if surgery is involved. And limitations to the amount of loss-of-income protection that can be purchased prevent its effectiveness as an all-encompassing insurance protection medium.

Loss-of-income insurance coverage is, however, basic coverage because no amount of hospitalization insurance will provide an income for your family when you are unable to work. If you do not work for a company that provides some form of salary continuance insurance, you should consider seriously the purchase of a loss-of-income insurance policy in addition to your hospitalization insurance plan.

Most plans available today provide for a wide variety of benefit periods (periods during which monthly benefits are payable), ranging from short six-month periods all the way to lifetime benefit periods. An ideal policy would pay lifetime benefits for disability due to accident, and benefits to age 65 for disability due to sickness, but such ideal plans

146

are expensive. Your present financial situation and salary continuance measures already in existence may suggest a compromise from the ideal plan, and in some cases may even dictate that no additional loss-of-income coverage is needed.

Although loss-of-income coverage can be purchased to provide benefits from the first day of disability, you could save considerably by purchasing a policy with *an elimination period*. Sometimes called waiting period, an elimination period begins on the first day of disability and effectively reduces the cost of protection because no benefits are payable during the period of time selected. If disability continues beyond the elimination period, benefits are paid beginning with the first day after the pre-selected elimination period ends. Elimination periods of 7, 14, 30, 60, and 90 or more days are normally available from which to choose. The longer the period, the lower the cost of the protection, but don't go overboard because benefits aren't payable until the period ends. You could find yourself in a financial bind meeting expenses that occur before the policy kicks in. Ideally, a 30-day elimination period is about right for a loss-of-income plan containing a benefit period of five years or less. Longer periods of elimination are generally recommended on lifetime policies, but keep in mind the fact that ideals may not meet your particular needs.

In addition to the primary monthly loss-of-income benefit, various supplemental benefits may be added to a policy. One benefit that has become popular in recent years is the *return of premium* benefit which, as the name suggests, returns to you all or a portion (usually 80% or more) of the premiums paid if there are no claims during a certain period of time. You can also add benefits for partial disability which provides for indemnity during a period of gradual return to work. Other benefits are available to cover medical expenses, loss of life or sight, and dismemberment.

The primary purpose of loss-of-income coverage is to provide a monthly income during periods of disability when you are not able to work. You should be aware of the fact that insurance companies do not agree on what constitutes a disabling condition, so definitions of disability (usually referred to as *total disability* in insurance policies) vary from one company to another. Some companies may require that you be "unable to perform any gainful employment whatsoever," some may require that you be "unable to return to any gainful employment for which you are reasonably qualified by education, training, or experience," and still others may utilize a composite of the two. The best plan would provide full benefits during the chosen benefit period until you are able to return to your regular job or, in the event you could not reasonably perform the same tasks as before, provide partial benefits (sometimes referred to as rehabilitative benefits) during the period it takes to learn another job — *and receive earnings* — for which you are qualified. Since the best plan will cost more, you will have to weigh the pros and cons with your particular situation and then choose the best plan that fits both your need and ability to pay.

Don't buy a plan that the company can cancel "at its option." Such plans could be cancelled just when you need the coverage most. Look for a plan that is at least guaranteed renewable to the earlier of (1) age 65 or (2) termination of employment. Most companies will not continue to insure you if you voluntarily quit working for obvious reasons, and benefits would be subject to reduction if your salary is reduced due to the salary-benefit limitation discussed earlier.

Finally, remember that you have a disability benefit entitlement under Social Security. Protection against loss of earnings due to disability became a part of Social Security in 1954 and applies to the majority of persons under age 65. There is a six month elimination (waiting) period on benefits under this federal program, meaning that benefits would not begin until the 7th full month of disability and the government's definition of disability is strict. The amount of your monthly disability benefit is based on average earnings under Social Security over a period of years, so the exact amount can't be figured in advance. Your local Social Security office can help you compute an estimate of this amount at your present age and salary conditions. By all means don't overlook this entitlement when you evaluate your loss-of-income insurance program.

There is a *rule of thumb* for determining loss-of-income insurance needs: reduce the amount of variable and fixed spending from your financial plan or budget as far as you possibly can. The result is equal to a close approximation of the minimum "salary continuance" income you will need in the event you are disabled and unable to work. Deduct from this amount the benefits you will receive from other salary continuance sources (group insurance from your job, welfare plans, and other programs), and the balance is the amount of loss-of-income coverage you need to maintain your present standard of living.

HEALTH INSURANCE
MINIMUM STANDARDS

Many states have adopted *minimum benefit standards* for health insurance. This means that insurance sold in these states after the date of adoption must meet the requirements of designated types of coverage, generally as follows: basic hospital and basic medical-surgical expense, major medical expense, hospital confinement indemnity, disability (loss-of-income), specified disease and specified accident, and accident-only. In most cases, policies that don't meet these minimums can be sold as limited or restricted benefit health insurance.

Although this is a noteworthy effort on the part of the states at benefit standardization, *no two states have exactly the same minimum standards*. These differences, in addition to meaning higher insurance premiums for all consumers, make it all but impossible to compare policies from one state to another or to draw specific conclusions with respect to the types of coverage sold. This fact is certain: *the burden of buying adequate coverage remains on the consumer.*

Whether you are buying coverage for the first time or evaluating coverage you already have, follow the guidelines described earlier in this chapter for assessing your insurance program. Buy only the coverage you need and be sure that the standards of your protection meet *your* minimums.

CHAPTER FOURTEEN

MEDICARE AND MEDICARE SUPPLEMENT INSURANCE

INTRODUCTION

The federal Medicare program, in spite of its much publicized funding problems, is one of the best insurance deals around. Established by Congress in 1965 through amendments to social security — the amendments constitute what is called *Title 18* — Medicare provides both hospital and medical insurance for virtually all citizens who are 65 years of age and over in this country.

Medicare does have deficiencies, but they can be easily remedied through the purchase of a good Medicare supplement insurance policy offered by insurance companies from coast to coast. Some are even offered by direct mail with no agent involved in the sale, and these plans are often excellent buys.

Many people make the mistake of buying too much insurance or too many policies thinking that "more" is "better." Oftentimes, the purchase of several Medicare supplement policies is encouraged by greedy sales agents who are more interested in high commissions than in the welfare of the prospective policyholder. One such case turned up in Missouri involved an 83 year old woman who had been induced by unscrupulous agents to purchase 13 such policies over a 5-year period. The case probably would not have come to light had she not experienced some difficulty meeting the monthly premium payments and sought advice from the state insurance department. Several agents representing several companies were involved in this scam, *and it is not just an isolated example.* The Federal Trade Commission has estimated that at least 25% of all senior-aged policyholders are overinsured. If the truth were completely known, that percentage would probably be much higher in this billion dollar per year insurance market.

Insurance counselors and advisors agree that *one good policy that fully supplements Medicare is enough extra insurance coverage for anyone.* Buying more than one policy is a waste of money, especially during inflationary times. The best way to decide what your Medicare supplement policy should provide in the way of benefits is to first determine what benefits Medicare doesn't provide, and then buy a plan that "fills in the gaps." Buying more coverage than you need may actually defeat the purpose for insurance in the first place if the insurance companies coordinate benefit payments with other coverages. Not only would you be deprived of additional benefits to meet expenses, you would be deprived of the money spent for premium payments, money that you certainly would need to meet other living expenses. *Don't buy more than one good policy.*

WHAT MEDICARE PROVIDES

There are two parts to the Medicare program. Part "A" provides *basic hospital insurance* protection, and is available to nearly everyone 65 years of age and over, and to many disabled people under age 65. Part "B" of Medicare provides *basic medical insurance* protection, and is available, on a voluntary basis, to the same age group as Part "A". These two parts of Medicare are discussed in detail below.

Medicare Part "A" (Hospital Insurance): During a *benefit period* (a benefit period begins when you enter the hospital and ends when you have been out of the hospital or skilled nursing facility for 60 consecutive days), Part A of Medicare pays as follows:

1. *First 60 days in the hospital:* All hospital costs except for the initial hospital expense deductible amount.

2. *61st through 90th day:* All hospital costs except a daily amount equal to one-fourth the hospital expense deductible in "1" above.

3. *91st through 150th day:* All costs except a daily amount equal to one-half the hospital expense deductible in "1" above. Called the *Lifetime Reserve*, this 60-day benefit can be used only once.

4. *Skilled Nursing Home:* All costs during first 20 days, and all costs except a daily amount equal to one-eighth the first hospital expense deductible for the next 80 days. You must be confined in a Medicare-recognized facility within 14 days of a hospital stay lasting at least 3 days.

5. *Home Health Care:* All health care worker visits (but not doctors), up to 100 visits in a 365 day period after a hospital stay lasting at least 3 days.

Note: The other deductibles, or coinsurance values, referred to above are calculated from the initial hospital expense deductible. In 1965, the initial deductible was $40. It is over five times that amount today with annual increases likely.

Medicare Part "B" (Medical Insurance): If you take this voluntary insurance (you don't have to, but you must decline it since the monthly premiums will be automatically deducted from your social security check), it covers most medical expenses and services of doctors and miscellaneous items not covered under Part "A". Except for the initial medical expense deductible in each calendar year, Part "B" of Medicare pays 80% of the reasonable charges for the following services:

1. *Physician's and Surgeon's Charges:* Services performed at home, doctor's office, or in the hospital.

2. *Outpatient Hospital Services:* Medical services and supplies, X-rays, laboratory tests, and similar services.

3. *Home Health Care:* Additional 100 days without the prior stay in the hospital requirement.

4. *Miscellaneous Medical Services:* Various expenses not covered under Part "A" are covered under Part "B".

BENEFITS OF A GOOD MEDICARE SUPPLEMENT POLICY

Assuming that you have decided that you *need* supplemental insurance to fill the gaps in Medicare coverage, you should look for a supplementing policy that fills those gaps in Medicare you wish to cover. For example, if you are in reasonably good health and can handle the initial hospital expense deductible currently in effect, you should probably consider looking for a plan that doesn't cover the initial deductible. By so doing, you may well save 50% or more over the cost of a plan that provides benefits covering this initial deductible.

You should also keep in mind that average hospital stays range from about 7 to 10 days, so be sure the plan you buy covers expenses that Medicare doesn't during that period. Some policies may not begin paying benefits until the 8th day of hospitalization. Of course, if you are financially able to handle expenses during such an initial period, you would save considerably in premiums. Policies that provide for initial waiting periods on benefits generally are not classified as true "Medicare supplement" policies. Instead, they provide flat-amount indemnity benefits which may or may not meet your needs.

A good Medicare supplement policy will also automatically keep pace with Medicare deductibles. When they increase, and they've increased over fivefold since 1965, your policy should increase automatically to meet them. Of course, your premiums will increase, but only nominally.

Don't wait for sickness to strike before applying for a Medicare supplement plan, because the very problem you are most likely to need coverage for may be excluded. Many such policies impose a six to twelve month waiting period for benefits covering old health problems (pre-existing conditions). Don't buy a plan that excludes old health conditions altogether or one that has a pre-existing waiting period longer than twelve months. You should be able to find a good plan that covers old health problems after a six month wait if you shop around.

The most popular Medicare supplement plan provides benefits that supplement both the hospital and medical expense portions of Medicare, but there are plans available in many states that supplement either portion. If your situation is such that dictates the purchase of Medicare supplement insurance, your best bet would be a plan that supplements both portions of the federal Medicare program. Based on Medicare deductibles in effect in 1982, you can expect to pay at least $500 per year for a plan giving full supplemental protection. This amount could be less if the plan is sold through the mail.

GUIDELINES FOR CHOOSING A MEDICARE SUPPLEMENT POLICY

Read the following guidelines carefully. They will help you choose a quality Medicare supplement plan that effectively meets your needs.

1. Evaluate your need for the coverage in relation to your financial situation.

2. Buy only one good policy from a reputable company licensed in your state.

3. Choose a policy that meets your needs. You will save money if you buy only the protection that your situation dictates.

4. Don't buy a plan that excludes pre-existing conditions altogether, or one that excludes them for more than twelve months (preferably six months).

5. Buy a plan that is guaranteed renewable for life, not one that the company reserves the right to nonrenew or cancel.

6. If you buy a plan through the mail, read the advertisement carefully and be satisfied that it provides all the protection you need.

7. If you buy a plan through an agent, be sure he is licensed in your state. Choose an agent carefully, and don't buy from anyone who tries to pressure you into it.

8. If you have questions about Medicare supplement insurance or about companies selling such plans, write or call the consumer division of your state insurance department. They will answer your questions and help you if you've got a problem, both before and after you purchase a plan.

9. If you are covered by group insurance that contains special "after age 65 benefits," you may not need additional coverage at all. Check with your insurance company or employer first.

10. **Ask questions.** Don't be afraid to ask questions about Medicare or Medicare supplement insurance. Ask friends, relatives, agents, insurance department personnel, your local Medicare office, anyone who can provide the information you need upon which to make wise decisions about your insurance needs and how to meet them. And don't buy coverage until you're satisfied that your questions have been answered.

Many states have now adopted minimum standards that apply to Medicare Supplement insurance. Most of the policies sold in these states cover all of the expenses of both Parts A and B that Medicare doesn't, *but you should shop around for the best deal.* Premium rates can and do vary between companies.

CHAPTER FIFTEEN

LIFE INSURANCE

THE PURPOSE OF LIFE INSURANCE

The primary purpose of life insurance is *to replace income lost when the income-producer dies.* In most cases, the income-producer is the head of the family. However, more and more families rely on two incomes to provide the funding required to meet financial obligations in today's society, and both incomes should be considered in terms of life insurance protection.

Most financial experts advise that a family *should* have life insurance coverage in an amount equal to no less than four or five years of disposable personal income. As salaries rise to meet inflation, the amount of life insurance needed goes up as well. Based on recent income averages, most of us are inadequately insured in the area of life insurance protection. A thorough understanding of the kinds of life insurance is essential, and will enable you to provide the amount and kind of life insurance protection needed in our inflation-prone world.

In addition to protecting present income, life insurance can be used *as a means of providing an income in old age.* Referred to as retirement income, endowment, and annuity plans, they are widely available but are not recommended as a means of providing an income for the informed consumer.

Savings and investments, earning much higher interest rates than even the best life insurance policies provide, should be the primary method of providing for income in retirement years. The informed consumer will use life insurance to protect present income, not to provide for income in old age.

KINDS OF LIFE INSURANCE

There are three basic kinds of life insurance (the fourth described is a variation of the first):

1. **Permanent or whole life plans:** These policies accumulate nonforfeiture values, also called cash values, which are guaranteed in the plan (meaning that you will not forfeit them if you should stop paying premiums after a certain period of time). Permanent life insurance pays the face amount benefit upon death of the insured person, regardless of when death occurs. There are a variety of premium payment periods available — single payment life, 10 year, 20 year, 30 year, to age 65, to age 95, or premiums payable for life (actuarially to age 100). Cash values accumulate in proportion to the premium payment period selected, and may be "borrowed" against in time of need at ridiculously low interest rates. Cash values may also be taken upon surrender of the policy or may be used to pay premiums in times of income shortage, pay for fully paid-up insurance in an amount the cash value permits, or pay for extended term insurance. See *variable interest plans* below.

2. **Endowment insurance plans:** These policies provide an endowment payable to the policyholder at some future date or maturity date agreed upon and stated in the policy. It is, in reality, a form of saving a sum of money for later use. Endowment plans will pay the endowment or amount of money saved to a beneficiary in the event the insured person dies before the maturity date of the policy. Endowment policies can not, to any realistic extent, provide a future sum to

158

the policyholder or beneficiary that could match savings or investments and are not recommended for the informed consumer.

3. **Term insurance plans**: Term life insurance accumulates no cash values, nor does it provide a means of saving for the future. In a very real sense, term insurance is *pure insurance* because premiums are based entirely on the probability of death occurring during the term of coverage. Term insurance is also referred to as temporary insurance, providing the most economical way to insure against the chance of untimely death during a certain period (term) of years. It is most often used to provide extra life insurance protection during the years when mortgage payments are made, children are growing up, and income is above average. For those individuals who have a well-established savings and investment program, term life insurance is traditionally used to protect against loss of present income exclusively. Such families would never purchase permanent or endowment insurance because they would be paying for something they don't need, and a portion of those payments would return (in savings growth) only a fraction of what they could otherwise accumulate in other, more productive savings mediums.

4. **Variable interest plans**: A few companies now offer life insurance with cash values tied to the business environment. If permanent life insurance fits your "lost income protection" needs, these flexible interest rate plans could be your best bet.

YOUR LIFE INSURANCE PROGRAM

Each person must develop a life insurance program *to fit his own special needs*. Age, income, family size, and financial position all play a part in developing the best life insurance program at the lowest possible cost. There is no set rule that applies equally to everyone. However, the following rule will help determine what is considered the *minimum* amount of life insurance protection the average family should have:

$$\text{Minimum Life Insurance Coverage} = \begin{matrix} \text{Sum Total of} \\ \text{Disposable} \\ \text{Family Income} \\ \text{From All} \\ \text{Sources During} \\ \text{Last 4 Years} \end{matrix}$$

Financial advisors do not all agree on this amount, but most agree that the minimum should be considerably more than the average "face amount" in force today. An amount equal to five years' disposable income is probably more realistic.

TERM vs. PERMANENT INSURANCE

Unless you are considerably more blessed financially than the average family, your life insurance program should consist of both term and permanent insurance. Term insurance provides pure life protection at low cost; permanent insurance builds cash values. How much of each to buy has been and always will be argued. There simply is no set rule — you must decide what your immediate needs are, what they will be in five years, ten years, and so on . . . and buy accordingly as further discussed below. Keep in mind that as family situations change, so too your life insurance program should change. Your decision today should be reevaluated as significant changes occur, *but at intervals of no less than once every two years.*

Theoretically, a person would be better off financially if he would invest, in a good savings or investment program, the amount of money he would save by buying term life insurance instead of permanent life insurance. The reason is simple: a savings program returning 6 to 8 percent is much greater than the 3½ to 4½ percent interest that goes into the makeup of most permanent life insurance cash values. However, most people will not faithfully invest the difference, and the compounding effect of life insurance cash values literally out-compounds the intermittent effect of inconsistent investing.

160

If you have the drive, determination, and willpower to faithfully invest, in a good savings or investment program on a monthly basis as discussed in other sections of this book, then by all means *buy only term life insurance.* If you can't or won't establish a solid savings and investment program, then consider seriously the purchase of permanent cash value insurance to cover that portion of the amount determined by using the "minimum life insurance coverage" formula discussed above that is not needed to cover temporary expenses. For example, the outstanding balance on your mortgage and money needed to educate children are temporary expenses. That portion of the amount calculated using the formula to cover temporary expenses should be covered by term insurance (for the term of the expense obligation).

Since the *net worth* of a family's estate in the event of the untimely death of the income-producer may reflect heavily on the proceeds of a life insurance program, buying term insurance instead of permanent insurance can more than double those proceeds. The reason? Term insurance gives more protection for the insurance dollar than permanent insurance. A carefully chosen term life plan can more than double those proceeds over what might be realized with permanent life insurance protection.

Assuming that you have the desire and determination to establish a solid savings and later investment program for your family's future well-being, buy only term life insurance. The money saved will go a long way toward building your financial estate, far greater than could be realized from cash values of permanent life insurance.

The following cost comparison between term and permanent life insurance is typical of the savings that can be achieved through careful planning and purchasing. The figures are for a male, age 35 years; the amount of insurance is $100,000:

Permanent to Age 65	**Five-Year Renewable** **Term to Age 62 Years**
$165.35 per month	$78.55 per month
(premium remains the same to age 65)	(average of all payments to age 62)

Remember that the primary purpose of life insurance is *to replace an income lost during income-producing years.* Which of the two policies do you believe most efficiently achieves that intended purpose? If you possess the financial means to buy the more expensive permanent plan, why not buy the term policy and invest the money you'd save in a high interest-paying savings or investment program?

LIFE INSURANCE FOR CHILDREN

There is considerable pressure today to start a financial program in the form of life insurance for children. Agents, direct mail, even school insurance brochures present a convincing picture of the virtues of and reasons for such "thoughtful protection for the little ones we love." Two commonly quoted reasons for the purchase are as follows: (1) *a matter of economics* — the earlier a life insurance program is started, the lower the total dollar outlay will be; and (2) *to protect insurability* — accidents and illnesses during childhood which might otherwise result in loss of insurability will not affect existing insurance protection.

The reasons given above comprise true statements, insofar as they apply to the question of buying life insurance at an early age; but they should *not* be interpreted as valid reasons for purchasing life insurance as a financial program. The purpose of life insurance in the first place is to protect a lost income, and it is doubtful that such purpose encompasses the domain of most children today (if it does, it's a different story).

Informed consumers begin a financial program for the benefit of children while their children are young, but in the form of savings and investments. You, to the ultimate benefit of your children, would be far better off doing the same.

Insurance bought wisely insures a wise person . . .

DETERMINE LIFE INSURANCE NEED, THEN BUY WISELY

It is possible to buy life insurance through the mail, where no agent is involved in the transaction, *but be wary.* You aren't going to get the best deal unless a medical application is taken and a physical examination is performed, and mail order insurers usually require neither. Mail order insurers do issue smaller "face amount" policies which could be utilized to supplement or up-grade existing coverage, but the rates per unit of coverage are generally higher to offset the bad risks they must expect and will surely get.

After you have made a careful determination of your family's life insurance needs and the kind of life insurance to buy, seek out a reputable, experienced agent who does business in your community. Shop around for an agent who is truly a professional in his field, one who has been in the business for several years, has a successful operation, and who faithfully services his accounts. Remember, your agent is the liaison between you and the insurance company. He should be chosen (not the other way around) with the same degree of care you would exercise in choosing a doctor, lawyer, stockbroker, or other competent advisor.

Don't sell your family's life insurance needs short. Evaluate your existing coverage candidly, determine whether it is realistically meeting the prospective needs of the family now and several years down the road, *and buy accordingly.* If your existing life insurance program is adequate, then channel additional funds into savings and investments. Never buy more life insurance than you truly need just because it may be in vogue. The money you will save by buying only what is needed will go a long way toward securing your family's financial future in the form of savings and investments.

CHAPTER SIXTEEN

AUTOMOBILE INSURANCE

INTRODUCTION AND COVERAGE SUMMARY

Automobile insurance is a combination of several different types of coverage serving special insurance needs. Understanding what each consists of will help you decide whether your present automobile coverage is adequate or inadequate, and provide you with some guides upon which to base future automobile insurance purchases. If your understanding and subsequent evaluation reveals deficiencies in existing coverage, it may even suggest that you find another insurance company to handle your automobile insurance needs.

There are *seven distinct types of coverage* associated with automobile insurance. A combination of all or several of these coverages comprise the automobile insurance "package." In order of discussion, they are: liability coverage, property damage coverage, medical payments coverage, collision coverage, comprehensive coverage, uninsured motorist coverage, and miscellaneous coverage which includes everything from coverage for towing disabled automobiles to coverage for accidental death.

1. **Liability coverage:** This coverage protects you, your family, and anyone driving your car with permission, against bodily-injury judgments when the person driving your car is legally liable for the accident. You and your family are also protected from such judgments while driving someone else's car with their permission. The coverage applies to the injuries to others, not to you, your family, or the one driving your car. Your insurance company need only agree that you were liable for the accident to compensate the other party or defend you in a suit (up to established limits discussed in the next section).

2. **Property damage coverage:** Coupled with bodily-injury liability coverage, your insurance company agrees to compensate, up to predetermined limits, for property damage losses incurred by the other party in the accident for which you, a family member, or any person permissibly driving your car, is responsible.

   The maximum amount your insurance company will pay for bodily-injury and property damage to others is stated in the policy, usually in this manner: $20,000/$40,000/$10,000. The first amount shown — $20,000 — is the maximum amount per person that your company will pay in any one accident; $40,000 is the maximum payable for all parties injured; and $10,000 is the maximum liability your company will assume for property damage to others. Remember, liability coverage protects you by paying for injuries and damages you cause to others. *It does not cover your injuries or damages.*

   All states have enacted liability insurance minimums which you must carry. If you live or drive in an urban area, these minimums are probably too low to be realistic. It doesn't cost much to increase liability coverage limits, and the wise consumer will carry liability limits at least equal to those prevailing in his own community.

3. **Medical payments coverage:** This coverage pays for medical and hospital expenses incurred by you and all passengers in your car, regardless of who was responsible for the accident. It also covers you and other family members while riding in someone else's car, or while walking. Medical payments coverage may be unnecessary if you are fully covered under your family hospitalization insurance program. Keep in mind that if the other party is responsible for the injury-causing accident, his liability coverage may pay your medical expenses.

   A wide range of medical payment maximums are available. Again, community practice based on regional costs should be considered when deciding what maximums are right for you. *Caution:* if you have no full-coverage family hospitalization insurance, buy medical payments coverage. The cost is small in relation to the benefits afforded.

4. **Collision coverage:** Usually sold in conjunction with a deductible — the higher the deductible, the lower the premium — collision coverage pays for damage to your car, regardless of who was at fault. Of course, if the other person caused the accident, his company may pay for your expenses. If not, yours will. Since your company will pay only an amount in excess of the deductible equal to the actual value of your car, it may not be worth it to buy collision coverage on an older car.

5. **Comprehensive coverage:** As the name implies, comprehensive coverage provides a broad range of protection for your car against perils other than accidents — windstorm, fires, flood, falling objects, theft, vandalism, collisions with animals, etc. It will also cover certain articles stolen from your car and pay for car rental if your car is stolen. Comprehensive coverage may not be needed on an older car, especially if your Homeowner's policy covers items stolen from it.

6. **Uninsured motorist coverage:** If you or a family

member are hit by an uninsured or hit-and-run motorist, uninsured motorist coverage will compensate you for medical expenses incurred. Usually, such compensation is limited to the state liability minimums of the state in which injury occurs and is payable (under this special coverage) only if you or your family member did not cause the accident. This coverage does not protect against property damage, however, except in a few states and then only under certain conditions.

7. **Miscellaneous coverages**: Various inexpensive coverages can be added to your policy to cover contingencies for which you may want added protection. Coverage for accidental death, dismemberment, and disability caused by an automobile accident may be desired if you use your car considerably or frequently drive long distances. The additional cost for the coverage is nominal. Many motorists buy towing and car disability coverage which provides for reimbursement of costs incident to breakdowns, flat tires, etc. If you decide to buy various miscellaneous coverages, be sure you aren't unnecessarily duplicating coverages provided in other insurance policies. Many Homeowner's policies provide car towing protection, as do all motor club memberships.

AUTOMOBILE INSURANCE RATING PRACTICES

A company's loss experience in a locality and the degree to which the state regulates premium rates go hand-in-hand toward determining what premiums you will pay for insurance in your community. Obviously, you'd expect to pay more for the same coverage in Boston than you would in Red Oak, Iowa, but you wouldn't want to pay significantly more for the same coverage in the same community. Unless you shop around for the best buy, you might wind up paying 20 to 30 percent more than you would by going with another, equally reliable company. If one company gets hit hard claimwise in an area, the policyholders will feel the crunch.

Individual rating practices vary, but most companies base their rating classifications on at least these variables: age of the insured, marital status, type and size of car, primary use of car (business, farmwork, pleasure), distance driven daily (urban or rural), and total distance driven in a year. Some companies offer good driver discounts, non-smoker discounts, driver's education discounts, and even good student discounts; if you or members of your family fit into these discount categories, don't overlook the savings possibilities.

Above all else, *compare rates of several different companies before you buy.* You may be pleasantly surprised at the savings you can realize just by shopping around. If you question the reliability of a prospective company, write or call your state insurance department. Or ask other policyholders of the company residing in your community.

Automobile insurance is most commonly sold through agents or brokers, but a few companies do solicit exclusively through the mail with no agent involved in the sale. Mail order rates may be lower, but you'd better be familiar with claim filing procedures if you go this route. You won't have an agent to petition on your behalf, and this can be a significant disadvantage to many people.

If you have or develop a bad driving record, you may not be able to buy "regular" automobile insurance coverage from any company. In such cases, your only resort may be to take coverage from an *assigned-risk pool* (arranged by your state) or *nonstandard company*, at least until you prove that your driving habits and record deserve consideration as a normal risk. The rates in such pools and nonstandard coverage companies can be extremely high and the coverage is bare minimal, especially in the assigned-risk pools. Stick it out and demonstrate a clean record for two or three years and you will probably be able to obtain regular coverage again.

NO-FAULT AUTOMOBILE INSURANCE

Many states have enacted some form of no-fault automobile insurance, and it is likely that all states will eventually have some form of no-fault legislation on the books.

The no-fault concept, proposed in 1966 and first adopted by the Commonwealth of Massachusetts in 1971, came into existence to accomplish two important things: (1) to provide immediate payments for medical expenses without waiting for the courts to allocate responsibility, and (2) to reduce insurance costs by eliminating the costly litigation resulting from and incident to automobile accidents.

If you live in a state where no-fault is in effect, your insurance company — regardless of who is at fault — will reimburse you for medical expenses up to certain limits which vary by state. If the other party is responsible for the accident, expenses in excess of these limits may be sought by taking action against the responsible party or his insurance company in the "fault" fashion. No-fault also provides for reimbursement for lost wages during periods of disability following an accident. If you sustain serious injury or if your medical expenses exceed a stipulated amount, you may be able to sue the responsible party for "pain and suffering." Some states permit such suits without regard to the seriousness of the injury or costs involved.

CHAPTER SEVENTEEN

HOMEOWNER'S INSURANCE

INTRODUCTION

Homeowner's insurance consists of a family of six policies called the homeowner series. Four of these policies cover homes, one covers apartments, and one covers condominiums. The coverage provided under these policies is virtually universal and easy to understand, but it has been estimated that 3 out of 4 homeowners/renters aren't sure what their policies cover until after a loss. This chapter will help you understand all of the policies in the series, and the coverage provided by each.

THE TRAGIC MISTAKE: UNDERINSURING REPLACEMENT COST

Before discussing insurance company requirements with respect to insuring replacement cost of a home, it is important that you understand the difference between replacement cost and market value. *Market value* of a home takes into account the value of the land, location of the property, improvements to the property, and appeal of the area. *Replacement cost* simply reflects the cost to replace the dwelling if it is destroyed.

Insurance companies generally require that a home be insured for 80% of its replacement cost in order for policy benefits to be realized fully in the event of loss. The 80% figure reflects the house exclusive of foundation, because it is assumed, for insurance purposes, that the foundation will survive almost any catastrophe and represents about 20% of the dwelling cost. For all practical purposes, a home insured for 80% of its replacement cost is fully covered.

As an example, let's assume fire completely destroys the roof of a house insured for 80% of replacement cost. What will the insurance company pay? They will pay the full replacement cost of the roof. If, on the other hand, the same house was insured for less than the 80% replacement cost figure, the company would pay only the greater of (1) the actual cash value of the roof (its replacement cost minus depreciation), or (2) a prorata amount based on the percentage coverage in effect.

Many companies offer an *inflation-guard rider* which automatically increases the face amount of coverage each year to keep pace with the increasing replacement cost of your home. The premium rises proportionately, of course, but the additional cost is usually quite reasonable. Even with the inflation-guard protection, you should evaluate your program every year or two just to make sure that the automatic increases are realistic for your home and area. Some may not be. An inflation-guard rider that increases coverage by 8% per year would add $10 to $15 to the annual premium on a $50,000 policy (80% coverage on a $62,500 replacement cost home), depending on location.

THE HOMEOWNER SERIES: CHOOSING THE RIGHT COVERAGE

The homeowner series consists of six policies: Forms HO-1, HO-2, HO-3 and HO-5 cover homes; Form HO-4 covers renters; and Form HO-6 covers condominiums. Of the four that cover homes, Broad Form HO-2 is by far the most popular because it generally offers the best coverage for the least money. All four of the home coverage plans cover damages to the house, garage (attached or detached), other outbuildings such as toolsheds and cabanas, furniture, appliances, and other personal property both on and off the premises. And they provide for temporary living expenses, personal liability claims against you or your family, medical expenses for injuries to others, and damage to the property of others.

There are limits to coverage (other than the house itself) expressed as a percentage of the face amount of coverage you buy. Detached garages and other outbuildings are covered up to 10% of policy value; furniture, appliances and other personal property, 50%; personal property off the premises, greater of $1,000 or 10% of policy value; temporary living expenses, 20% of policy value (10% on Form HO-1).

Some limits of coverage are expressed as a dollar figure: personal liability, $50,000; medical payments, $500 per person up to $25,000 per accident; damage to property of others, $250. There is also a $250 allowance to cover the service charge assessed by the fire department.

All of the limits described above apply to Homeowner Forms HO-4 (renters) and HO-6 (condominium owners), except as follows: there is no coverage on the apartment or condominium itself, or on garages or other outbuildings; furniture and other personal property is 100% covered; temporary living expenses for condominium owners is provided at 40% of policy value; and there is no coverage for fire department service charges.

The perils covered by the six Homeowner Forms are described below:

Basic Form HO-1. ....Fire, hail, lightning, windstorm, explosion, riots, aircraft, glass breakage, vandalism, smoke, theft, and vehicles other than your own.

173

Broad Form HO-2. ...Same as HO-1 plus building collapse, damage from weight of ice, snow and sleet, freezing, accidental damage to or from heating or plumbing systems, damage by electrical equipment, and falling objects.

Special Form HO-3. ..Covers all perils except earthquake, landslide, mud flow, floods, tidal waters or waves, war, nuclear radiation, sewer backup and seepage. House contents and personal property off-premises are covered as under HO-2 above only.

Comprehensive Form HO-5. ....Coverage is the same as under HO-3, except coverage also applies equally to house contents and personal property off-premises.

Renters Form HO-4. ....The apartment itself is not covered, but furniture, appliances, and other on- or off-premises personal property is covered to the same extent as under HO-2.

Condominium Form HO-6. ....Same perils as under HO-4.

Obviously, Form HO-1 provides the least coverage for the homeowner, HO-5 the most. Forms HO-3 and HO-5 are considered "all risk" coverage as far as the house itself is concerned, but they could be deficient if, for example, you live in an area frequented by one of the excluded perils. Since these perils are also not covered under Broad Form HO-2, many homeowners choose to buy the less expensive Form HO-2 plan and purchase a "rider" or supplemental policy designed to cover only the potentially disasterous peril.

It is possible (and often wise) to increase certain limits of coverage within the policy itself. For example, if the 50% limit on personal property is insufficient to cover the loss of all your personal possessions, it can be increased by paying an additional premium. Many companies today offer *item-for-item replacement cost* protection on personal property either in the policy or available as an option. However, some items may require coverage by separate policy or rider since there are special limits of liability which apply to specifically-named items (e.g., jewelry, furs, securities, boats and trailers).

Broad Form HO-2 will generally provide adequate protection for the average homeowner, assuming that 80% of the replacement cost is insured. Most policies contain a $100 deductible. You could save about 10% on your annual premium by increasing the deductible to $250; you would save about 20% if the deductible is increased to $500. Regardless of what size deductible you decide is right for your coverage needs and financial situation, *don't insure your house for less than 80% of its current replacement cost.* And reevaluate that figure periodically, at least every two years.

Some companies will allow a 5% premium reduction if your home is protected by smoke and burglar alarms. If you do have such devices installed in your home, check out the savings potential with several insurance companies.

If you should suffer a catastrophic loss involving most or all of your household possessions, some insurance companies may require that you present an itemized listing of everything — yes, *everything* — that you lost. You should keep an inventory of your personal belongings, and the inventory, or at least a copy of it, should be kept in a safe deposit box or some other safe place off the premises. Many agents advise their policyholders to take pictures of each room in their house from several vantage points since some companies will accept them in lieu of an itemized listing of personal property. Whatever method of inventory you use, by all means don't rely on memory to recall every gidget and gadget that you own. Write it down or take pictures, and keep your inventory records in some other location. And update your inventory as situations and possessions change.

APPENDIX

FIGURE 2-01: FINANCIAL WORKSHEET. Use this chart format to record income and expense data for the prior year (or other period of equal duration to planning period chosen). Be as accurate as possible. Omit nothing. Your figures will be used to project income and expenses most likely to occur during your planning period.

INCOME

	ANNUAL*	Monthly
TAKE-HOME INCOME, all sources	$_____	$_____
INCOME from interest, dividends, etc.	_____	_____
OTHER INCOME	_____	_____
TOTAL	$_____	$_____

EXPENSES

	Annual*	Monthly
FIXED EXPENSES		
Taxes not withheld from Income	$_____	$_____
Money saved	_____	_____
Money invested	_____	_____
Insurance premiums _____	_____	_____
(Types of coverage) _____	_____	_____
_____	_____	_____
Mortgage or rent	_____	_____
Loan payments	_____	_____
Other credit payments	_____	_____
TOTAL FIXED EXPENSES:	$_____	$_____
VARIABLE EXPENSES		
Food and beverages	$_____	$_____
Utilities: Gas or oil	_____	_____
Electricity	_____	_____
Telephone	_____	_____
Water and sewer	_____	_____
Household operation and maintenance	_____	_____
Transportation: Automobile expenses	_____	_____
Public transportation	_____	_____
Clothing	_____	_____
Medical care	_____	_____
Dental care	_____	_____
Gifts and contributions (charity)	_____	_____
Educational expenses	_____	_____
Personal expenses	_____	_____
Special expenses	_____	_____
Miscellaneous expenses	_____	_____
TOTAL VARIABLE EXPENSES:	$_____	$_____
TOTAL EXPENSES, Fixed and Variable:	$_____	$_____

*Other period if different from annual

179

FIGURE 2-03: IMPORTANT FAMILY FINANCIAL GOALS. Realistic and reasonable family goals, and your plan for financial achievement of each, should be recorded on a chart similar to the one below.

YOUR GOALS	TARGET DATE	APPROXIMATE DOLLAR VALUE	COST/MO.
SHORT-RANGE GOALS			
INTERMEDIATE-RANGE GOALS			
LONG-RANGE GOALS			

FIGURE 2-04: FINANCIAL PLAN. Use this chart format to record income and expenses most likely to occur during your planning period. Base projections on worksheet data evaluated against realistic and reasonable family goals, past money management practices, and your commitment to effectively and efficiently use family resources.

PROJECTED INCOME

	Annual*	Monthly
TAKE-HOME INCOME, all sources	$_____	$_____
INCOME from interest, dividends, etc.	_____	_____
OTHER INCOME	_____	_____
TOTAL	$_____	$_____

PROJECTED EXPENSES

	Annual*	Monthly
FIXED EXPENSES		
Taxes not withheld from Income	$ _____	$_____
Financial Security: Savings	_____	_____
Investments	_____	_____
Life Insurance	_____	_____
Health Insurance	_____	_____
Automobile Insurance	_____	_____
Homeowner/apartment Insur.	_____	_____
Mortgage or rent	_____	_____
Loan payments	_____	_____
Other credit payments	_____	_____
TOTAL FIXED EXPENSES:	$_____	$_____
VARIABLE EXPENSES		
Food and beverages	$_____	$_____
Utilities: Gas or oil	_____	_____
Electricity	_____	_____
Telephone	_____	_____
Water and sewer	_____	_____
Household operation and maintenance	_____	_____
Transportation: Automobile expenses	_____	_____
Public transportation	_____	_____
Clothing	_____	_____
Medical care	_____	_____
Dental care	_____	_____
Gifts and contributions (charity)	_____	_____
Educational expenses	_____	_____
Personal expenses	_____	_____
Special expenses	_____	_____
Miscellaneous expenses	_____	_____
TOTAL VARIABLE EXPENSES:	$_____	$_____
TOTAL EXPENSES, Fixed and Variable:	$ _____	$_____

*Other planning period if different from annual

FIGURE 2-05: NET WORTH STATEMENT

Net Worth Satement

Year: _____

ASSETS

Cash: amount on hand	$_____
savings accounts	_____
checking accounts	_____
House, current market value	_____
Other real estate, market value	_____
Household furnishings, value	_____
Automobile, current retail value	_____
Life insurance, cash value	_____
Stocks and bonds, current value	_____
Money owed you	_____
Other assets	_____
TOTAL	$_____

LIABILITIES

Mortgages, balance due today	$_____
Installment debts, balance due	_____
Credit card purchases, balance due	_____
Charge accounts, current balance	_____
Other debts, total amount owed	_____
TOTAL	$_____

NET WORTH

Assets minus liabilities	$_____

INDEX